ALBERT EINSTEIN'S "WHY SOCIALISM?"

Albert Einstein's "Why Socialism?"

The Enduring Relevance of His Classic Essay

edited and with an introduction by
John Bellamy Foster

MR

MONTHLY REVIEW PRESS
New York

Library of Congress Cataloging-in-Publication Data
available from the publisher.

ISBN 978-1-68590-099-1 cloth

Typeset in Bulmer Monotype

MONTHLY REVIEW PRESS, NEW YORK
monthlyreview.org
5 4 3 2 1

Contents

Preface

Albert Einstein's "Why Socialism?" first published seventy-five years ago in *Monthly Review* is one of his most popular works, greatly admired by socialists and radicals around the world. Many readers are of course attracted to Einstein's essay simply by his enormous scientific reputation and the respect he is accorded as a result. Oddly, this has resulted in his article often being treated as an anomaly. Despite its fame there are few serious commentaries on his article, which is usually read divorced from its historical context, and by readers who have little or no knowledge of Einstein's extensive contributions to socialism throughout his life and its relation to his conception of science. This small volume is thus designed to make Einstein's essay readily available, while providing the larger political and historical context in which it can be understood.

In the introduction to this work, "Einstein's 'Why Socialism?' and *Monthly Review*," I have sought to provide a framework for reading his article. This includes not only a discussion of Einstein's role as a socialist, but also the hitherto unknown history of the series of events that led up to the publication of his article in *Monthly Review* in May 1949. In addition, commentary is provided on Einstein's article to explain the bases on which his argument was constructed. Some space is devoted also to accounting for obvious distortions of Einstein's "Why Socialism?" appearing in academic treatments that seek to remove many of the more rebellious aspects of his analysis, subtracting from rather than adding to his vision.

The introduction is followed by Einstein's article itself in an easily readable copy, taking up twelve pages, as opposed to the little more than six in its first publication. In this way, this remarkable work is highlighted as the classic it is.

Finally, an afterword includes John J. Simon's notable treatment, "Albert Einstein, Radical: A Political Profile," written for *Monthly Review* in May 2005, on the occasion of both the fiftieth anniversary of Einstein's death and the centennial of his "miraculous year" in which he published five epoch-making scientific papers, establishing his world reputation. Simon's elegance of style and historical sense have made his essay unsurpassed in revealing the inner character of Einstein's political life.

It is hoped that this slim volume will bring Einstein's "Why Socialism?" to life for generations both old and new. Its relevance has only grown in the three-quarters of a century since it was written. To ask, "Why Socialism?" as Einstein did in his day, is to raise the question of the future of humanity.

— JOHN BELLAMY FOSTER
EUGENE, OREGON
JULY 24, 2024

Einstein's "Why Socialism?"
and *Monthly Review*: A Historical Introduction

by John Bellamy Foster

A Spring 1949 memorandum in the Federal Bureau of Investigation's "Albert Einstein File," part of the FBI's *Vault* of documents released under the Freedom of Information Act, states:

> Advised [by an agent in the field that] in April 1949, a circular was distributed in the Nashua, New Hampshire area, announcing a new magazine entitled "Monthly Review," "an independent Socialist magazine." The first issue was dated to come out as the May 1949 edition. The first issue would contain articles by Albert Einstein—"Why Socialism[?]"; Paul M. Sweezy—"Recent Development[s] in American capitalism"; Otto Nathan—"Transition to

11

Socialism in Poland"; Leo Huberman—"Socialism and American Labor.". . . Re: New York report, dated 3–15–51 Espionage-CH.[1]

The rest of the message is blacked out. Another memorandum that immediately follows in the FBI's Einstein file, and which is similarly redacted, reads:

Advised the New York Office that the "Monthly Review" 66 Barrow Street, New York City, self-proclaimed "an independent Socialist magazine" made its initial appearance in May of 1949. The first issue contained articles by Albert Einstein and others. This [investigative] report stated further that a study of the articles contained in a background check of the editors and contributors revealed that this magazine was Communist inspired and followed the approved Communist Party line. . . . New York report, dated 1-30-50; Re: Internal Security.[2]

Albert Einstein, the world's most famous theoretical physicist and its most celebrated scientist, had fled Germany upon Adolf Hitler's rise, immigrating to the United States in 1933, where he became a citizen in 1940. Yet, for J. Edgar Hoover's FBI, Einstein remained a dangerous and Un-American figure, threatening the internal security of the United States by his very presence in the country. His publication in May 1949 of an article titled "Why Socialism?"

for the new periodical *Monthly Review: An Independent Socialist Magazine* was thus viewed by the FBI as a direct confirmation of his strong "Communist sympathies."

The FBI had opened its file on Einstein in 1932, when he was seeking to immigrate to the United States, with a long report by the Woman Patriot Corporation (WPC), which in its extreme anti-Communism, claimed that Einstein was inadmissible to the country. "*Not even Stalin himself*," the WPC charged, "is affiliated with so many anarcho-communist international groups to promote . . . world revolution and ultimate anarchy, as ALBERT EINSTEIN."[3] The FBI continued to collect everything it could on Einstein's numerous socialist connections for the remainder of his life.[4]

Although Einstein famously sent a letter to President Franklin D. Roosevelt on August 2, 1939, on the possibility of developing an atomic bomb—a letter that has often been seen as directly leading to the Manhattan Project—the U.S. military declared him a security risk, and he was excluded from the development, and even knowledge, of the making of the atomic bomb during the Second World War, including the decision by President Harry S. Truman to drop it on Hiroshima and Nagasaki.[5]

In the late 1940s, the Red Scare associated with McCarthyism, named after U.S. Senator Joseph McCarthy, was already beginning. In April 1949, only a month before Einstein's "Why Socialism?" was published in *Monthly*

Review, *Life* magazine (*Time* magazine's sister publication), included Einstein in a two-page photo spread of fifty leading "Dupes and Fellow Travelers" of Communism in the country. The spread also included such celebrated figures as composer and conductor Leonard Bernstein, actor Charlie Chaplin, poet Langston Hughes, playwright Lillian Hellman, U.S. Congressman Vito Marcantonio, American studies professor F. O. Matthiessen, playwright Arthur Miller, atomic physicist Philip Morrison, writer Dorothy Parker, and radio commentator J. Raymond Walsh. Former U.S. vice president Henry A. Wallace was portrayed on the previous page as a "standout fellow traveler."[6]

No doubt adding to the FBI's fears and suspicions at the time, connected to the general anti-Communist hysteria, was the fact that Einstein's "Why Socialism?" made one of the most succinct and powerful cases for socialism ever written. It is an essay that has stood the test of time, and which is far more celebrated worldwide today, seventy-five years later, than it was at the date of its publication.

"In this Sense, I Am a Socialist"

Einstein in 1949 was no new initiate to socialism. In 1895, aged 16, he had moved to Switzerland to study at Zürich's Federal Polytechnic School.[7] For Einstein, 1905 was to be the "miraculous year," during which he received his PhD at the University of Zürich and published five breakthrough papers in theoretical physics (including his doctoral dissertation) that were to make him world-famous. He was to be revered worldwide as a personification of human progress and creativity.

But Einstein's creativity as a scientist and his universalism were never separate from his commitment to a more egalitarian society. He was a convinced socialist, connected to innumerable radical groups and causes, and a dedicated opponent of all forms of discrimination. After its opening in 1911, he spent a great deal of time hanging out at the Grand Café ODEON in Zurich, which was a meeting place for Russian radicals, among them Alexandra Kollontai, and, later, V. I. Lenin and Leon Trotsky, along with numerous avant-garde cultural figures. He was undoubtedly caught up in the many fiery political-cultural discussions taking place there. Nor was his a timid socialism. He saw the need in certain historical circumstances for revolutions. On November 19, 1918, the day that Kaiser Wilhelm II abdicated, Einstein famously posted on his classroom door: "CLASS CANCELED—REVOLUTION."[8] A year later he wrote: "I do advocate a planned economy . . . in this sense I am a socialist."[9] In 1929, he stated: "I honor Lenin as a man who completely sacrificed himself and devoted all his energy to the realization of social justice. I do not consider his methods practical, but one thing is certain: men of his type are the guardians and restorers of the conscience of humanity."[10] In a 1931 article, "The World as I See It," he wrote: "I regard class distinctions as unjustified, and, in the last resort, based on force."[11] Reflecting his strong commitments to socialism and workers' education, Einstein delivered lectures in the early 1930s to the Marxist Workers School in Berlin.[12]

Although he subsequently was to distance himself from the Soviet character of the organization, Einstein, along with Bertrand Russell, Upton Sinclair, and other independent socialists, signed on to the broad stance of the International Congress Against Imperialist Wars in 1932.[13] In 1945 he declared: "I am convinced . . . that in a state with a socialist economy the prospects are better for the average individual to achieve the maximum degree of freedom that is compatible with the well-being of the community."[14]

As Einstein's close friend and associate Otto Nathan was to explain in *Einstein on Peace* in 1960:

> Einstein was a socialist. He believed in socialism because, as a convinced equalitarian, he was opposed to the class division in capitalism and to the exploitation of man by man which he felt this system facilitated more ingeniously than any previous economic organization. He was a socialist because he was certain that a capitalist economy could not adequately perform for the welfare of *all* people and that the economic anarchy of capitalism was the source of many evils in contemporary society.

And, finally, he was a socialist because he was convinced that, under socialism, there was a greater possibility of attaining the maximum degree of freedom compatible with the public welfare than under any other system known to man.[15]

The Albert Einstein Foundation and the Rise of McCarthyism in Higher Education

In 1933, Einstein joined the newly established Institute for Advanced Study in Princeton. Here he was to spend a great deal of time with Nathan, who was a visiting professor in the Princeton economics department and who, like Einstein himself, was a refugee from Nazi Germany. Nathan, a socialist economist, had received his doctorate in economics and law in Germany in 1921, and was an economic adviser in the Weimar government. In the United States, he had served in 1930–31 on President Herbert Hoover's Emergency Committee on Employment. He resigned his posts in Germany in 1933 and was hired as a visiting lecturer at Princeton in 1933–35, after which he taught at New York University from 1935–42, at Vassar from 1942–44, and at Howard University from 1946–52. Nathan lectured on Marxist economics to the Marxist Study Group at Vassar in the early 1940s. He worked closely with Einstein from 1933 until the latter's death in 1955, often also serving as a financial adviser.

Einstein referred to him as his "closest friend" and confidant. Nathan was sole executor and co-trustee (along with Einstein's secretary, Helen Dukas) of the Einstein estate. During their long collaboration, Einstein treated Nathan as his representative on political and educational issues, emphasizing their accord on all questions.[16]

For Einstein, a humane, progressive education was directly linked to the advancement of the socialist cause. In 1946–47, he was to play a prominent role, together with Nathan, in the founding of Brandeis University, originally conceived as a Jewish-based secular institution of higher learning that would also represent a new, broader conception of a free university. Here, Einstein's views of educational reform and radical social change were to come together. The founding of Brandeis was a response to the quota system in the U.S. Ivy League institutions, as well as almost all other colleges and universities, restricting the number of Jewish students, along with those of other minorities.[17] The original proposal for the new university was to name it after Einstein, but he declined and declared that it should be named instead after "a great Jew who was also a great [native-born] American," which led to the naming of the university after former U.S. Supreme Court justice Louis Brandeis.[18] Nevertheless, Einstein's support was crucial in getting the new university off the ground. The main funding source for the institution of the new university was the Albert Einstein Foundation for Higher

Learning, the board of which included Nathan. The chairman of the Foundation was S. Ralph Lazrus, a wealthy businessman with a progressive political outlook, who was tied to the department store chain Allied Stores and the Benrus Watch Company. Brandeis's Board of Trustees was chaired by George Alpert, a conservative Boston lawyer, president of the Boston and Maine Railroad, and a leading figure in Jewish philanthropy.[19]

In January 1947, Paul M. Sweezy, one of the world's most prominent left economists, author of *The Theory of Capitalist Development: Principles of Marxian Political Economy* (1942)—who had just stepped down from his position as a professor of economics at Harvard—submitted an eighty-seven-page report titled *A Plan for Brandeis University* outlining a proposed structure for the new university.[20] The Sweezy plan was clearly commissioned by the Albert Einstein Foundation, emanating from Nathan as Einstein's representative. Nathan and his good friend, socialist labor journalist Leo Huberman, met almost daily while the former was teaching at New York University. As a result, Nathan had become acquainted with Sweezy, with whom Huberman had a strong friendship and a close working relationship.[21] Sweezy's role as a founder of the Harvard Teacher's Union in the 1930s no doubt influenced the decision to have him write the plan for Brandeis.

Sweezy's Brandeis plan was aimed at creating a more open, accessible, and forward-looking university, unlike any then existing in the United States. It had "two major premises." First, "the heart and soul of the university" would be "its faculty," who would govern the university themselves as the ultimate authority. All standards and incentives should be determined from within, rather than coming from without. Second, the university itself would be conceived as "a *community* of scholarship and learning." Sweezy indicated that the emphasis should be placed on establishing a first-rate small institution, commencing with a faculty of one hundred and a student body of around five hundred. The initial emphasis would be the social sciences and humanities, with the faculty organized into schools, not departments. He also underlined that priority be given to "attracting qualified Negroes for both faculty and student body" and that a certain number of scholarships offered by the university be set aside "exclusively for Negro students." These proposals were all in line with the views of Nathan and Einstein, with Nathan putting forward a five-page outline of the structure of the new university with which the more extensive Sweezy plan dovetailed. A key critical work singled out in Sweezy's *A Plan for Brandeis University* was Thorstein Veblen's *The Higher Learning in America*.[22]

A conflict, however, was to arise between the Albert Einstein Foundation for Higher Learning and the Brandeis Board of Trustees over the Foundation's progressive academic plans. This was to come out into the open in the context of selecting a president for the new university. In search of a potential president, and with Einstein's support, Nathan went to London to meet with Harold Laski, no doubt encouraged by Huberman and Sweezy, both of whom had studied under Laski at the London School of Economics (LSE).[23] Laski, a former Harvard instructor, then for many years a professor at the LSE, and a member of the executive of the British Labour Party, was widely recognized as one of the world's leading political-economic thinkers. In 1939, Laski wrote an article, "Why I Am a Marxist," originally published in the United States in *The Nation* and later reprinted in *Monthly Review* upon his death in 1950. Responding to the Great Depression and the rise of Nazism, he declared: "The time has come for a central attack on the structure of capitalism. Nothing less than wholesale socialization can remedy the position. The alternative in all Western civilization . . . is, I believe, a rapid drift to fascism."[24]

Nathan and Einstein believed that Laski, as one of the leading Jewish thinkers in the world, committed to secular education and displaying strong socialist values, was the ideal choice for the president of Brandeis, able to shape the freer, more open, and more progressive university that they envisioned. Einstein, with the initial support of Alpert, and with what Einstein understood was the authorization of both the Board of Trustees and the Foundation (though this was to be questioned later), wrote to Laski, inviting him to consider taking up the position as president of Brandeis.[25] In his April 15, 1947, letter, Einstein said:

Dear Mr. Laski,

As you have learned from my friend, Mr. Otto Nathan, a few months ago, a very serious effort is being made here to found a new University which we feel has become necessary because of the quota system openly or subtly used by almost all American Colleges and Universities. We hope that the new institution will make it easier for young men and women of Jewish faith and of other minorities to obtain a first-class education. Similarly, we hope to make it possible for those scientists and scholars, who under present conditions suffer from grave discrimination, to find a place where they can teach and work. The University will be in Jewish hands, but we are determined to develop it into an institution which is enlivened by a free, modern spirit, which emphasizes, above all, independent scholarship and research and which does not know of discrimination for or against anybody because of sex, color, creed, national origin or political opinion. All decisions about education policies, about the organization of teaching and research will be in the hands of the faculty.

The Board of Trustees has delegated to me the authority of selecting the first president of the University. This man would have the challenging task to help us in determining the basic foundation of the University and to select and organize the initial faculty upon whom so much depends. We all feel that among all living Jews you are the one man who, accepting the great challenge, would be most likely to succeed. Not only are you familiar with the United States and her academic institutions more intimately than many American educators, your reputation as an outstanding scholar is widespread throughout the country.

I am writing, therefore, to ask you whether you would be prepared to consider such an invitation.[26]

Laski responded almost immediately to Einstein's offer, indicating that, unfortunately, for personal and family reasons, as well as his commitment to the struggle for socialism in Britain, he was unable to leave London, and therefore he could not accept the position.[27] However, despite Laski's letter declining the position, which had already been received, Alpert clearly saw the Laski offer as a potentially contentious issue, and a way of seizing control of the university's direction. The goal was to marginalize Nathan and Lazrus, and therefore Einstein, by nullifying the role of the Albert Einstein Foundation in the determination of the academic direction of the university. Thus, despite his initial support for the offer to Laski, Alpert now took the opposite tack. He suddenly claimed, though the charge was a dubious one with no clear evidence to support it, that Nathan and Lazrus (indirectly implicating Einstein himself) had exceeded their authority in making such an offer to Laski. Alpert denied that the Board of Directors of the Foundation had authorized the offer in a meeting, which he now declared had lacked a quorum.[28] More to the point, he insisted that the Laski choice was unacceptable because it reflected radical "Un-American" politics. Einstein's response was to defend Nathan and Lazrus, and to make it clear that they had his full confidence and had acted in line with his own views. He emphasized that it was he himself who had written the letter to Laski after first getting the approval of Alpert, the Board of Trustees, and the Foundation. Einstein then severed his connection to Brandeis, arranging for the name of the Albert Einstein Foundation for Higher Learning to be changed to the Brandeis Foundation, with both Nathan and Lazarus resigning their positions.

According to Alpert, whose remarks on the incident were highlighted by the *New York Times* on June 23, 1947, under the headline "Left Bias Charged in University Row," Einstein's associates had "arrogated to themselves the shaping of academic policy" aiming to give the university "a radical political orientation," and "surreptitiously" making overtures to a "thoroughly unacceptable choice." In Alpert's words, "To establish a Jewish-sponsored University and to place at its head a man utterly alien to American principles of democracy, tarred with the Communist brush, would have condemned the University to impotence from the start.... On the issue of Americanism I cannot compromise." Other newspapers picked up the story, claiming that Laski was objectionable as an "international socialist of record."[29] It was no mere coincidence that Alpert's political allegations were entirely in accord with the views of the National Council for American Education, a fervently anti-Communist organization founded in 1946 that launched McCarthyism in the universities. With the introduction of McCarthyite tactics, Alpert was declaring that it was unacceptable for any intellectual figure associated with socialist ideas to head a U.S. university.[30]

Einstein was shocked at the red-scare tactics being used against him and his associates, as indicated in his draft response to Alpert's public statements. His actual public response, however, was restrained and to the point:

The press statements which Mr. George Alpert and another member of the Board of Trustees of Brandeis University released on the occasion of the withdrawal of myself and of my friends, Professor Otto Nathan and Mr. S. Ralph Lazrus, have convinced me that it was none too early for us to sever a connection from which no good was to be expected from the community. My associates and myself had very reluctantly come to the conclusion that the type of academic institution in which we have been interested could not be accomplished under the existing circumstances and present leadership.[31]

As William Zuckerman wrote in the Jewish publication *The American Hebrew*: "Mr. Alpert's statement is ... [that] of a narrow partisan reactionary politician behooving a member of the Un-American Activities Committee, not a president of a university named after the late Justice Brandeis."[32]

The Wallace Campaign and the Birth of Monthly Review

The failure in the repressive climate of the time to establish a new kind of open, democratic university dedicated to a more progressive vision, one with absolute control over the institution being exercised by the faculty, lacking racial discrimination in its admissions policies, and incorporating socialist values of equality, had a deep effect on Einstein. In 1948, in the midst of the anti-Communist hysteria that was then being directed against all left-wing movements in the country, including the radical-labor, civil rights, and left-academic forces that had formed a coalition during Roosevelt's New Deal, Einstein threw his support behind Wallace, the Progressive Party candidate in the presidential election. Wallace had the support of the radical forces that had provided much of the impetus for Roosevelt's New Deal. His campaign opposed the Cold War, supported international control of nuclear weapons, and backed civil rights and the rights of labor. A famous photo taken shortly before the official launching of the Progressive Party shows Einstein and Paul Robeson standing next to Wallace.[33] Huberman and Sweezy wrote the preamble to the Progressive Party platform, which was adopted at the Philadelphia Convention in July 1948. Sweezy was to take on the position of chairman of the Wallace campaign in New Hampshire.[34]

Although garnering over a million votes, Wallace lost decisively in the election, partly due to the red-baiting campaign directed against him by the Democratic Party presidential candidate, then-President Truman.[35] In the wake of Wallace's disastrous defeat, Huberman, Sweezy, Nathan, and seemingly Einstein as well, concluded that a key reason for Wallace's dismal electoral showing was a failure to articulate a positive vision, which could only come from socialism. Einstein believed that Wallace was "without doubt a liberal," not a socialist.[36]

Under these circumstances, Huberman, Sweezy, and Nathan were convinced that what was needed in the United States was an independent socialist periodical that would provide the necessary political education and vision, even if this was only to be, in the context of the times, a mere "holding action, a rearguard action."[37] Consequently, they began to work together to found what became *Monthly Review*. They were helped by Matthiessen, who had worked with Sweezy in the 1930s in forming the Harvard Teacher's Union and was also an active supporter of Wallace. He provided the magazine with a critical $5,000 in each of its first three years.[38] Nathan was a silent member of the founding editorial team of the new magazine, not wanting to be on the masthead given the McCarthyite attacks already being directed at university professors. He wrote for the first two issues of *Monthly Review* and was heavily involved in its planning and development. However, his role was gradually to recede in the initial year of publication. His most lasting contribution to *Monthly Review* was to encourage Einstein to write for the first issue.[39]

Hence, when the inaugural issue of *Monthly Review* was published in May 1949, Huberman and Sweezy were listed as editors, while the four authors of articles in the issue (following two editorials) were Einstein, Sweezy, Huberman, and Nathan, in that order. It was Einstein's article in the first issue of *Monthly Review* that took on the main task of articulating the meaning of socialism itself and drew the FBI's attention to the magazine.

There was a longstanding tradition of major socialists publishing articles titled "Why I am a Socialist."[40] Nathan, with the support of Huberman and Sweezy, suggested to Einstein that he write an essay of this kind. Einstein, however, decided to adopt an entirely different format, not based on his own subjective views, but rather making a straightforward objective case for choosing a socialist path, leading to the very distinctive quality of "Why Socialism?," which took on a scientific character.[41]

Einstein and the Objective Case for Socialism

Written with desperate brevity, Einstein's "Why Socialism?" was just over six pages long in its original printing. Although uniquely his own product, it showed the influence of two great socioeconomic thinkers: Veblen and Karl Marx. As C. Wright Mills famously wrote in an introduction to Veblen's *The Theory of the Leisure Class*, "Thorstein Veblen is the best critic of America that America has produced."[42] In the 1940s, Veblen was one of Einstein's favorite authors. In 1944, Einstein wrote, "I owe innumerable happy hours to the reading of [Bertrand] Russell's works, something which I cannot say of any other contemporary scientific writer, with the exception of Thorstein Veblen."[43] Einstein saw Marx as a great thinker, whom he ranked alongside Baruch Spinoza as an exponent of human freedom arising from the Jewish tradition. As he declared: "Embedded in the tradition of the Jewish people there is a love of justice and reason which must continue to work for the good of all nations now and in the future. In modern times this tradition has produced Spinoza and Karl Marx."[44]

Albert Einstein's "Why Socialism?"

The first half of "Why Socialism?" was related to Veblen's views. Einstein commenced his essay with the question and answer: "Is it advisable for one who is not an expert on economic and social issues to express views on the subject of socialism? I believe for a number of reasons it is." He proceeded to explain that up to the present day "nowhere have we overcome what Thorstein Veblen called 'the predatory phase' of human development. . . . Since the real purpose of socialism is precisely to overcome and advance beyond the predatory phase of human development, economic science in its present state can throw little light on the socialist society of the future."[45] It was also the case that socialism was "directed towards a social-ethical end" to which science, as normally understood, could contribute little. Hence, experts on current economic arrangements were not "the only ones who have a right to express themselves on questions affecting the organization of society."[46]

Einstein's principal occupation at this time was the struggle for world peace in the face of the existential threat represented by nuclear weapons. The question of peace was directly connected to the relation of the individual to society. The typical individual in contemporary capitalism was so alienated and distraught by the dire circumstances then prevalent, both economic in origin and arising from the threat of war, so as frequently to question the very concept of humanity. As Einstein wrote, "I recently discussed with an intelligent and well-disposed man the threat of another war, which in my opinion would seriously endanger the existence of mankind, and I remarked that only a supra-national organization would offer protection from danger. Thereupon my visitor, very calmly and coolly, said to me: 'Why are you so deeply opposed to the disappearance of the human race?'"[47]

Nothing else, Einstein stated, so clearly pointed to the contemporary social and moral crisis: "I am sure that as little as a century ago no one would have so lightly made a statement of this kind. It is the statement of a man who has striven in vain to attain an equilibrium within himself and has more or less lost hope of succeeding. It is the expression of a painful solitude and isolation from which so many people are suffering in these days. What is the cause? Is there a way out?"[48] The very refusal of individuals to face up to the existential crisis facing humanity in the nuclear age, going so far as to deny the importance of the continuation of human existence, dramatized the despair and alienation that was then—as now—rife, necessitating a search for a *way out*.

"Man," Einstein observed in "Why Socialism?," "'is at one and the same time a solitary being and a social being." The character of the human being is thus a product of both individual and social drives, reflecting inward and outward forces.[49] Each person has both an inherited "biological constitution" and a "cultural constitution" adopted from society, which together affect one's development. Nevertheless, individuals are able to influence their own lives to some extent by virtue of consciousness, communication, and the actions each chooses to take within the constraints presented by society, which is itself subject to change. "The social behavior of human beings may differ greatly, depending upon prevailing cultural patterns and the types of organization which predominate in society. It is on this that those who are striving to improve the lot of man may ground their hopes: human beings are *not* condemned, because of their biological constitution, to annihilate each other or to be at the mercy of a cruel, self-inflicted fate."[50]

It was this strongly held conviction that led Einstein in his essay to address the structure of present-day society. The dependence of the individual on society today, he wrote, is such that the individual "does not experience this dependence as . . . an organic tie, as a protective force, but rather as a threat to his natural rights, or even to his economic existence." This is because the structure of society is such as to accentuate "the egotistical drives" and at the same time to weaken the "social drives" in the individual's makeup, "which are by nature weaker," thus going against the insurmountable fact that "man can find meaning in life, short and perilous as it is, only through devoting himself to society."[51]

Relying on Marx for much of his argument at this point, Einstein emphasized that while there is "a huge community of producers" in today's "capitalist society," the vast majority of these are deprived "of the fruits of their collective labor," since "the entire productive capacity of society" is "for the most part . . . the private property of individuals." Here, he outlined "for the sake of simplicity" (that is, at a high level of abstraction), the main characteristics of a capitalist class society. In such a system, "the 'workers' . . . [or] all those who do not share in the ownership of the means of production" are compelled to sell their "labor power" to "the owner of the means of production."[52] The owner is thus in a position to appropriate the entire surplus (value) generated beyond what is first paid to the worker in order to meet the "minimal needs" of the latter. "It is important to understand," he wrote, "that even in theory the payment of the worker is not determined by the value of his product."[53]

The main contradictions of capitalist class society, according to Einstein, stemmed from its promotion of inequality. Rather than tending toward egalitarian conditions, "private capital tends to become concentrated in few hands" through the normal operation of the accumulation process, whereby "the formation of larger units of production" occurs "at the expense of smaller ones." This generates "an oligarchy of private capital" that is so powerful that "it cannot be effectively checked even by a democratically organized society." This is all the more the case since elected politicians and the parties to which they belong are "largely financed or otherwise influenced by private capitalists" who stand between the electorate and the greater part of the population. "Moreover, under existing conditions, private capitalists inevitably control, directly or indirectly, the main sources of information (press, radio, education)," which mediate between those who rule the society and the population as a whole.[54]

Capitalism, Einstein explained, is a system in which "production is carried on for profit, not for use," leaving many underprivileged and underserved. The system is supported by "an army of unemployed," so that the worker is constantly fearful of being cast back into the reserve army of labor. New technological developments often result in workers being thrown out of work, thereby further enhancing the army of the unemployed and the relative power of the owners.[55] "The profit motive," together with unrestrained competition, are responsible for severe economic crises, a "huge waste of labor," and the "crippling of the social consciousness of individuals." The last is "the worst evil of capitalism," since it allows society to be turned against the population. "Our whole educational system" cultivates such alienated values, and thus "suffers from this evil."[56]

"I am convinced there is only *one* way to eliminate these grave evils," Einstein declared, "namely through the establishment of a socialist economy, accompanied by an educational system which would be oriented toward social goals. In such an economy, the means of production are owned by society itself and are utilized in a planned fashion" in line with social, as well as individual, needs. "The education of the individual, in addition to promoting his own innate abilities, would attempt to develop in him a sense of responsibility for his fellow men in place of the glorification of power and success in our present society."[57] Here we see the importance that he placed, as expressed in his letter to Laski, on the creation of a higher education institution free of "discrimination for or against anybody because of sex, color, creed, national origin, or political opinion"—one in which "all decisions about education policies, about the organization of teaching and research will be in the hands of the faculty," not boards of trustees filled with business magnates.

"A planned economy," Einstein insisted, "is not yet socialism." It does not necessarily mean the end of "the enslavement of the individual." The actual achievement of socialism meant addressing crucial issues such as the questions of extending rather than limiting democracy, combating bureaucracy, and protecting the rights of the individual. He ended his article by referring to *Monthly Review*, the founding of which he strongly backed: "Clarity about the aims and problems of socialism is of greatest significance in our age of transition. Since, under present circumstances, free and unhindered discussion of these problems has come under a powerful taboo, I consider the foundation of this magazine to be an important public service."[58]

The "powerful taboo" was the McCarthyism then dominating the entire discourse of U.S. society. Einstein himself had felt its force directly in his attempts to create a new, freer university in Brandeis that fell prey to charges of Un-Americanism; in his role in the Wallace campaign, which led to his being castigated as a "dupe and fellow traveler" of Communism; and in the witch-hunt style attacks on many of the socialists and radicals with whom he was most closely associated. Although Einstein's world reputation and status made him virtually untouchable, this was not true of the other authors who wrote for the first issue of *Monthly Review*. Huberman, Sweezy, and Nathan were all to be called up before the McCarthyite inquisition and threatened with prison for their refusal to name names and cooperate. They rested their cases on the First Amendment, as famously recommended by Einstein.[59]

"Why Socialism?" or "Why Liberalism?"

Such is the power of Einstein's name and the force of his views that even today, seventy-five years after the publication of "Why Socialism?," efforts are being made to deny or downplay his commitment to socialism, and to argue that "Why Socialism?" was of little importance, did not say what it seemed to say, was contradicted by his own intellectual development, and has no real significance for our times. Most biographical treatments of Einstein simply ignore his politics altogether as of little consequence.[60] In reality, this has to do with the inconvenient fact that Einstein was a political radical, often seen as a tribune of the left.

However, in recent years, interest in Einstein's political views has greatly increased as a result of Fred Jerome's publication in 2002 of *The Einstein File*, which recorded the FBI's pursuit of him for his left political views. In 2007, authors David E. Rowe and Robert Schulmann, both noted Einstein scholars, published the edited collection *Einstein on Politics* with Princeton University Press. The book was quickly recognized as an invaluable resource, bringing together materials from numerous sources, some of them previously unpublished. Rowe and Schulmann not only provided a general introduction but also extensive commentary on the various items included in their collection.

The most obvious deficiency of the Rowe and Schulmann book was the exclusion of Einstein's many treatments of racism outside the questions of Judaism, Zionism, Israel, and Palestine. "Only after the [Second World War]," they wrote, did Einstein begin "to speak out more insistently about the enduring legacy of slavery manifested in white America's feelings of superiority toward blacks." Here, though, they were forced to qualify this by acknowledging that Einstein had written on racism in the United States as early as 1931–32, while nonetheless leaving out the crucial fact that the key article referred to was written for *The Crisis* magazine under the editorship of none other than W. E. B. Du Bois.[61] Only Robeson, not Du Bois, appears in Roe and Schulmann's account of Einstein's politics—and even then, Robeson is mentioned only in relation to the famous photograph of him with Einstein and Wallace.[62]

Yet there is another, more subtle deficiency in *Einstein on Politics*, related to the political agenda of the book, which is designed to transform Einstein from a socialist into a liberal. Here, Rowe and Schulmann seek to turn Einstein's most famous statement on socialism, "Why Socialism?," inside-out. Indeed, Einstein's "Why Socialism?," Rowe and Schulmann claim, despite its title, was actually not a case for socialism at all, but rather for a kind of left-liberalism. Implicit in this is the idea that "Why Socialism?" should have been entitled "Why Liberalism?" Thus, they sharply criticize Nathan, Einstein's closest friend and confidant and the executor/trustee of his estate, for completely misunderstanding Einstein in describing him as a socialist.[63] "Why Socialism?," we are led to believe, may appear to be making a case for socialism, but this is soon dispelled if "properly contextualized."[64]

One part of this "*proper contextualization*," apparently, derives from the observation that Einstein was frequently critical of the Soviet Union, and had indicated in a letter that some Bolshevik theories were "ridiculous"—as if this in itself meant the wholesale rejection of socialism.[65] Moreover, a "*proper contextualization*" of "Why Socialism?," the editors of *Einstein on Politics* implausibly argue, includes the recognition that in criticizing "the oligarchy of capital," Einstein's intention was, in their words, "not so much to advance socialism as an economic system but to advocate a planned economy as a significant instrument for achieving social-ethical ends." Here they circumvent Einstein's own clearly stated view that a planned economy was a *necessary*, "socialistic" first step, if not a *sufficient* one, in the overall process of the creation of complete socialism.[66]

Because Einstein believed in human rights and democracy, it is oddly presumed by the editors of *Einstein on Politics* that he could not, therefore, have been a socialist. Thus, we are told that his arguments in "Why Socialism?" against "income inequality and the exploitation of the economically vulnerable," which he attributed to the capitalist system, if "*properly contextualized*," could be seen as falling "within the traditional liberal goal of self-realization of the individual," concerned with democratic rights—rather than constituting, as Einstein himself thought, arguments for democratic socialism.[67]

Turning to the question of intellectuals and the working class, the defenders of a "*proper contextualization*" of Einstein's politics proclaim that as an intellectual he had no direct experience with working-class conditions or with the working class itself, and thus necessarily "placed his faith in appeals to reason by a liberal intelligentsia"—as if *faith in appeals to reason by a socialist intelligentsia* were simply out of reach to him. Rowe and Schulmann appear to have been unaware of Einstein's lectures to the Marxist Workers School in Berlin. Although Einstein's direct connections to the working class were few, he was surrounded by socialists who did not lack such connections.[68]

In a further attempt to turn Einstein's politics inside-out, Nathan's straightforward declaration that Einstein was a socialist because of the his deep commitment to egalitarianism is subjected to a fierce attack by Rowe and Schulmann. They claim that Nathan, despite his close friendship with Einstein, mistook the real character of the great man, who was actually prone to a "fervent elitism."[69]

Finally, it is subtly suggested that a *"proper contextualization"* of Einstein's views in "Why Socialism?" would see him as a naïve "moral philosopher," unable to find his way in the real world of politics, leading to his utopian advocacy of a socialist future while belying his own innate liberal tendencies.[70]

Not only is Einstein (together with Nathan) subjected in this way to Rowe and Schulmann's *"proper contextualization,"* but so is the publication in which "Why Socialism?" appeared, *Monthly Review*. Rowe and Schulmann allege that the editors of *Monthly Review*, Huberman and Sweezy (and Nathan behind the scenes), "tried to appropriate" Einstein for their own leftist ends by publishing "Why Socialism?" "with great fanfare" in May 1949. Yet, far from "great fanfare," the *only* comment on Einstein or his article by anyone in the inaugural issue of *Monthly Review* in which his article appeared was a single line identifying the author: "Albert Einstein is the world-famous physicist."[71] His article was neither given top billing inside the magazine, since it followed two major editorials, nor was it highlighted on the cover. Rather than appropriating him "with great fanfare," the editors of *Monthly Review* might be reasonably criticized for having understated the signal importance of Einstein's essay.

The sense that the distinguished editors of *Einstein on Politics* would no doubt like to convey is that Einstein was far from being a willing participant in all of this. Such a view, however, is belied by his close relations to Nathan; his indirect connections to Sweezy in the planning of Brandeis; the roles that Huberman, Sweezy, and Einstein all played in the Wallace campaign; and the final paragraph of his article indicating strong support for the new magazine.

Not content with the above charges, Rowe and Schulmann go on to declare, as if to cast aspersions on the further "appropriation" of his essay, that the Einstein article had been reprinted by *Monthly Review* "every year" over its history. Yet, over the monthly magazine's then fifty-eight years of publication, at the time that Rose and Schulmann were writing, the Einstein article had only been reprinted in its pages eight times, approximately once every seven years.[72]

The Constant Political Struggle for Socialism

Einstein's advocacy of socialism was entirely at one with his positions on education, racism, colonialism, and peace. The red-baiting in relation to his plans for Brandeis University, his socialist commitments, and his letter to Laski has continued into this century.[73] Yet, in general, Brandeis has preferred to play down the political conflict, presenting Einstein as simply a magnanimous figure involved in the founding of the university and implying his continual support in order to better use his name.[74]

Einstein almost always politely declined offers from universities for honorary degrees, not only because these were so numerous, but also because he was uncomfortable with the nature of higher education in the United States.[75] But when offered such an honorary degree by the first president of Brandeis, Abram L. Sachar, in May 1953, he did not send his usual polite response, but angrily explained that "What happened in the stage of preparation of Brandeis University was not caused by a misunderstanding," but was deceptive and unconscionable "and cannot be made good any more." In an earlier reply in July 1949 to an overture from Sachar, he referred to "the untrustiness and untruthfulness of certain of the Board of Trustees" that had led to his severing all connections with the university.[76]

Yet, while Einstein deplored the way universities in

the United States, including Brandeis, were governed by business and elitist political interests, he was willing to accept such an honorary degree in 1946 from the small, historically Black, Lincoln University in Pennsylvania, which, when chartered in 1854, was the first institution of its kind. In his speech on that occasion, as reported in the *Baltimore Afro-American* (the mainstream press in general ignored his speech), Einstein said: "My trip to this institution was on behalf of a worthwhile cause. There is separation of colored people from white people in the United States. That separation [segregation] is not a disease of colored people. It is a disease of white people. I do not intend to be quiet about it." In a closely related article in January 1946 on "The Negro Question," Einstein declared: "The social outlook of Americans . . . their sense of equality and human dignity is limited to men of white skins. . . . The more I feel an American, the more this situation pains me. I can escape complicity in it only by speaking out." In response to a nationwide wave of lynching that year, he joined Robeson as co-chair of the American Crusade to End Lynching, despite the FBI's characterization of it as a Communist-front organization.[77]

In 1951, the federal government indicted Du Bois, then chairman of the Peace Information Center based in the United States, along with four other officers of the Center, for failing to register as "foreign agents." The Peace Information Center was charged with having circulated the

Stockholm Appeal of 1950 of the World Peace Council, which was classified by U.S. authorities as a Soviet-front organization.[78] The Stockholm Appeal was aimed at banning nuclear weapons and was signed by several million people. In federal court, Du Bois was defended by the fiery radical attorney and congressman, Vito Marcantonio.[79] Einstein had agreed to testify on Du Bois's behalf, but Marcantonio, in order to achieve the maximum effect, held back this information until the last moment—when he was about to call the defense witnesses. As Du Bois's wife, Shirley Graham Du Bois, recalled that day in court:

> The prosecution rested its case during the morning of November 20. . . . Marcantonio . . . told the judge that only one defense witness was to be presented, Dr. Du Bois. [But] Marcantonio added casually to the judge, "Dr. Albert Einstein has offered to appear as a character witness for Dr. Du Bois." Judge [Matthew F.] McGuire fixed Marcantonio with a long look, and then adjourned the court for lunch. When court resumed, Judge McGuire . . . granted the motion for acquittal.[80]

It was clear that the international publicity that would have ensued from putting Einstein on the witness stand in defense of Du Bois was too much for the judge, who dismissed the case on lack of evidence, even before Einstein could take the stand.[81]

Einstein deplored U.S. imperialism. As he wrote to the Queen Mother of Belgium, Elisabeth, in 1955: "I cannot rid myself of the thought that this, the last of my fatherlands, has invented for its own use a new kind of colonialism, one that is less conspicuous than the colonialism of old Europe. It achieves domination of other countries by investing American capital abroad, which makes those countries firmly dependent on the United States. Anyone who opposes this policy or its implications is treated as an enemy of the United States." He firmly believed that the United States was principally responsible for the tragedy of the Korean War.[82]

Einstein's well-known commitment to Zionism is often used as a way of denying or circumventing his radical and socialist views. A *Time* article titled "Einstein's Complicated Relationship to Judaism" by Samuel Graydon, published on December 19, 2023, in the midst of the continuing Israeli war on Gaza, claimed that Einstein was an out-and-out Zionist and "overcame his instinctive objections to the nationalist element inherent in the movement—that is the creation of a Jewish state." This, however, is a myth created almost immediately upon his death, designed to hide the truth.[83] Rather than explore the issue fully, which would raise difficult questions, the *Time* article quickly deviated into the details of Einstein's immigration to the United States and his supposed patriotic Americanism, despite the McCarthyite attacks on him, linking this fabled Americanism with his "commitment to the Zionist cause," on which, we are told, he "did not waver in his later years."[84] In fact, Einstein was consistently opposed to the creation of a "Jewish state" in Israel, arguing instead for a "binational" state including both Jews and Palestinians. Einstein was thus what has been referred to as a "cultural Zionist" as opposed to "political Zionist." He argued that Jewish immigration should be limited to what was compatible with the peaceful integration of Jews and Palestinians in a common homeland.[85]

Completely missing from the *Time* article was any reference to the December 8, 1948, letter to the *New York Times*, signed by Einstein, Hannah Arendt, Sidney Hook, Seymour Melman, and other Jewish intellectuals, warning of the rise in Israel of Menachem Begin's Herut ("Freedom") Party, the progenitor of today's Likud under Benjamin Netanyahu. The letter by Einstein and his cosignatories characterized Begin's Freedom Party as "a political party closely akin in its organization, methods, political philosophy and social appeal to the Nazi and Fascist parties."[86] The near total destruction of Gaza by the Israeli Defense Forces following Al-Aqsa Flood on October 7, 2024, leading, as of April 2024, to more than a hundred thousand casualties, including more than thirty thousand deaths—most of them women, children and other noncombatants—with many times that number facing starvation, has brought renewed worldwide attention to Einstein's warning on the evolution of the Israeli state.[87]

Einstein's principal concern in his later years was the threat of human annihilation due to nuclear weapons. In 1946 he became chair of the Emergency Committee of Atomic Scientists (ECAS). Other than Einstein, all of the committee members had worked on the development of the atomic bomb. Many were Nobel Prize recipients. Yet, the FBI was to list the ECAS as a Communist-front group, because of its efforts to remove atomic development from the military and put it under international control at a time when the United States still had a monopoly on nuclear weapons.[88]

On March 1, 1954, the United States carried out a disastrous hydrogen bomb test, code-named "Castle Bravo," on Bikini Atoll in the Marshall Islands. Intended to be an explosion with a yield of six megatons, it turned out, due to an error in calculation by the scientists involved, to be the largest nuclear explosion ever conducted by the United States, amounting to fifteen megatons—one thousand times the explosive power of the bomb dropped on Hiroshima. The fallout extended over eleven thousand square kilometers, falling on the Marshallese populations of the inhabited atolls and on a Japanese fishing boat eighty-two miles away, outside the official danger zone. When the boat, *Lucky Dragon*, made its way back to Japan, it was discovered that the fishermen were suffering from radiation sickness. News of this quickly reached Einstein and deeply affected him. Although the Eisenhower administration tried to hide the full extent of the disaster for a year, scientists began asking questions and providing their own data, forcing the administration to release much of its information. The result was enormous worldwide concern about the dangers of nuclear fallout from above-ground nuclear testing, along with the nuclear arms race in general. This was to lead to the massive struggle of scientists and citizens over the following years to enact the Nuclear Test Ban Treaty, signed in 1963, marking the first great success of the modern environmental movement, which started with concerns over atmospheric nuclear testing.[89]

Einstein's last signed statement, in April 1955, only days before his death, was in support of what has become known as the "Russell-Einstein Manifesto," which declared that "the best authorities are unanimous in saying that a war with H-bombs might quite possibly put an end to the human race. It is feared that if many H-bombs are used there will be universal death. . . . We urge the governments of the world to realize, and to acknowledge publicly, that their purposes cannot be furthered by a world war, and we urge them, consequently, to find peaceful means for the settlement of all matters of dispute between them."[90] As Einstein stated in "Why Socialism?," the attempt to find a "way out" from the threat of human extinction leads in the direction of socialism.

Einstein's commitment to socialism did not rest simply on the socialization of the means of production and the creation of a planned economy. Rather, he believed that "Socialism . . . requires that concentrated power be under the effective control of the citizenry, so that the planned economy benefits the entire population. . . . Only constant political struggle and vigilance can create and maintain such a condition." Indeed, "to tire in that struggle" for democracy and human rights, which could only be achieved fully under socialism, "would mean the ruin of society."[91] To the last, Einstein considered himself, in his own words, a political "revolutionary . . . a fire-belching Vesuvius," struggling on behalf of a common humanity.[92]

Why Socialism?

Is it advisable for one who is not an expert on economic and social issues to express views on the subject of socialism? I believe for a number of reasons that it is.

Let us first consider the question from the point of view of scientific knowledge. It might appear that there are no essential methodological differences between astronomy and economics: scientists in both fields attempt to discover laws of general acceptability for a circumscribed group of phenomena in order to make the interconnection of these phenomena as clearly understandable as possible. But in reality such methodological differences do exist. The discovery of general laws in the field of economics is made difficult by the circumstance that observed economic phenomena are often affected by many factors which are very hard to evaluate separately. In addition, the experience which has accumulated since the beginning of the so-called civilized period of human history has— as is well known—been largely influenced and limited by causes which are by no means exclusively economic in nature. For example, most of the major states of history owed their existence to conquest. The conquering peoples established themselves, legally and economically, as the privileged class of the conquered country. They seized for themselves a monopoly of the land ownership and appointed a priesthood from among their own ranks. The priests, in control of education, made the class division of society into a permanent institution and created a system of values by which the people were thenceforth, to a large extent unconsciously, guided in their social behavior.

But historic tradition is, so to speak, of yesterday; nowhere have we really overcome what Thorstein Veblen called "the predatory phase" of human development. The observable economic facts belong to that phase and even such laws as we can derive from them are not applicable to other phases. Since the real purpose of socialism is precisely to overcome and advance beyond the predatory phase of human development, economic science in its present state can throw little light on the socialist society of the future.

Second, socialism is directed towards a social-ethical end. Science, however, cannot create ends and, even less, instill them in human beings; science, at most, can supply the means by which to attain certain ends. But the ends themselves are conceived by personalities with lofty ethical ideals and—if these ends are not stillborn, but vital and vigorous—are adopted and carried forward by those many human beings who, half unconsciously, determine the slow evolution of society.

For these reasons, we should be on our guard not to overestimate science and scientific methods when it is a question of human problems; and we should not assume that experts are the only ones who have a right to express themselves on questions affecting the organization of society.

Innumerable voices have been asserting for some time now that human society is passing through a crisis, that its stability has been gravely shattered. It is characteristic of such a situation that individuals feel indifferent or even hostile toward the group, small or large, to which they belong. In order to illustrate my meaning, let me record here a personal experience. I recently discussed with an intelligent and well-disposed man the threat of another war, which in my opinion would seriously endanger the existence of mankind, and I remarked that only a supra-national organization would offer protection from that danger. Thereupon my visitor, very calmly and coolly, said to me: "Why are you so deeply opposed to the disappearance of the human race?"

I am sure that as little as a century ago no one would have so lightly made a statement of this kind. It is the statement of a man who has striven in vain to attain an equilibrium within himself and has more or less lost hope of succeeding. It is the expression of a painful solitude and isolation from which so many people are suffering in these days. What is the cause? Is there a way out?

It is easy to raise such questions, but difficult to answer them with any degree of assurance. I must try, however, as best I can, although I am very conscious of the fact that our feelings and strivings are often contradictory and obscure and that they cannot be expressed in easy and simple formulas.

Man is, at one and the same time, a solitary being and a social being. As a solitary being, he attempts to protect his own existence and that of those who are closest to him, to satisfy his personal desires, and to develop his innate abilities. As a social being, he seeks to gain the recognition and affection of his fellow human beings, to share in their pleasures, to comfort them in their sorrows, and to improve their conditions of life. Only the existence of these varied, frequently conflicting, strivings accounts for the special character of a man, and their specific combination determines the extent to which an individual can achieve an inner equilibrium and can contribute to the well-being of society. It is quite possible that the relative strength of these two drives is, in the main, fixed by inheritance. But the personality that finally emerges is largely formed by the environment in which a man happens to find himself during his development, by the structure of the society in which he grows up, by the tradition of that society, and by its appraisal of particular types of behavior. The abstract concept "society" means to the individual human being the sum total of his direct and indirect relations to his contemporaries and to all the people of earlier generations. The individual is able to think, feel, strive, and work by himself; but he depends so much upon society—in his physical, intellectual, and emotional existence—that it is impossible to think of him, or to understand him, outside the framework of society. It is "society" which provides man with food, clothing, a home, the tools of work, language, the forms of thought, and most of the content of thought; his life is made possible through the labor and the accomplishments of the many millions past and present who are all hidden behind the small word "society."

It is evident, therefore, that the dependence of the individual upon society is a fact of nature which cannot be abolished—just as in the case of ants and bees. However, while the whole life process of ants and bees is fixed down to the smallest detail by rigid, hereditary instincts, the social pattern and interrelationships of human beings are very variable and susceptible to change. Memory, the capacity to make new combinations, the gift of oral communication have made possible developments among human beings which are not dictated by biological necessities. Such developments manifest themselves in traditions, institutions, and organizations; in literature; in scientific and engineering accomplishments; in works of art. This explains how it happens that, in a certain sense, man can influence his life through his own conduct, and that in this process conscious thinking and wanting can play a part.

Man acquires at birth, through heredity, a biological constitution which we must consider fixed and unalterable, including the natural urges which are characteristic of the human species. In addition, during his lifetime, he acquires a cultural constitution which he adopts from society through communication and through many other types of influences. It is this cultural constitution which, with the passage of time, is subject to change and which determines to a very large extent the relationship between the individual and society. Modern anthropology has taught us, through comparative investigation of so-called primitive cultures, that the social behavior of human beings may differ greatly, depending upon prevailing cultural patterns and the types of organization which predominate in society. It is on this that those who are striving to improve the lot of man may ground their hopes: human beings are not condemned, because of their biological constitution, to annihilate each other or to be at the mercy of a cruel, self-inflicted fate.

If we ask ourselves how the structure of society and the cultural attitude of man should be changed in order to make human life as satisfying as possible, we should constantly be conscious of the fact that there are certain conditions which we are unable to modify. As mentioned before, the biological nature of man is, for all practical purposes, not subject to change. Furthermore, technological and demographic developments of the last few centuries have created conditions which are here to stay. In relatively densely settled populations with the goods which are indispensable to their continued existence, an extreme division of labor and a highly-centralized productive apparatus are absolutely necessary. The time—which, looking back, seems so idyllic—is gone forever when individuals or relatively small groups could be completely self-sufficient. It is only a slight exaggeration to say that mankind constitutes even now a planetary community of production and consumption.

I have now reached the point where I may indicate briefly what to me constitutes the essence of the crisis of our time. It concerns the relationship of the individual to society. The individual has become more conscious than ever of his dependence upon society. But he does not experience this dependence as a positive asset, as an organic tie, as a protective force, but rather as a threat to his natural rights, or even to his economic existence. Moreover, his position in society is such that the egotistical drives of his make-up are constantly being accentuated, while his social drives, which are by nature weaker, progressively deteriorate. All human beings, whatever their position in society, are suffering from this process of deterioration. Unknowingly prisoners of their own egotism, they feel insecure, lonely, and deprived of the naive, simple, and unsophisticated enjoyment of life. Man can find meaning in life, short and perilous as it is, only through devoting himself to society.

The economic anarchy of capitalist society as it exists today is, in my opinion, the real source of the evil. We see before us a huge community of producers the members of which are unceasingly striving to deprive each other of the fruits of their collective labor—not by force, but on the whole in faithful compliance with legally established rules. In this respect, it is important to realize that the means of production—that is to say, the entire productive capacity that is needed for producing consumer goods as well as additional capital goods—may legally be, and for the most part are, the private property of individuals.

For the sake of simplicity, in the discussion that follows I shall call "workers" all those who do not share in the ownership of the means of production—although this does not quite correspond to the customary use of the term. The owner of the means of production is in a position to purchase the labor power of the worker. By using the means of production, the worker produces new goods which become the property of the capitalist. The essential point about this process is the relation between what the worker produces and what he is paid, both measured in terms of real value. Insofar as the labor contract is "free," what the worker receives is determined not by the real value of the goods he produces, but by his minimum needs and by the capitalists' requirements for labor power in relation to the number of workers competing for jobs. It is important to understand that even in theory the payment of the worker is not determined by the value of his product.

Private capital tends to become concentrated in a few hands, partly because of competition among the capitalists, and partly because technological development and the increasing division of labor encourage the formation of larger units of production at the expense of smaller ones. The result of these developments is an oligarchy of private capital the enormous power of which cannot be effectively checked even by a democratically organized political society. This is true since the members of legislative bodies are selected by political parties, largely financed or otherwise influenced by private capitalists who, for all practical purposes, separate the electorate from the legislature. The consequence is that the representatives of the people do not in fact sufficiently protect the interests of the underprivileged sections of the population. Moreover, under existing conditions, private capitalists inevitably control, directly or indirectly, the main sources of information (press, radio, education). It is thus extremely difficult, and indeed in most cases quite impossible, for the individual citizen to come to objective conclusions and to make intelligent use of his political rights.

The situation prevailing in an economy based on the private ownership of capital is thus characterized by two main principles: first, means of production (capital) are privately owned and the owners dispose of them as they see fit; second, the labor contract is free. Of course, there is no such thing as a *pure* capitalist society in this sense. In particular, it should be noted that the workers, through long and bitter political struggles, have succeeded in securing a somewhat improved form of the "free labor contract" for certain categories of workers. But taken as a whole, the present day economy does not differ much from "pure" capitalism.

Production is carried on for profit, not for use. There is no provision that all those able and willing to work will always be in a position to find employment; an "army of unemployed" almost always exists. The worker is constantly in fear of losing his job. Since unemployed and poorly paid workers do not provide a profitable market, the production of consumers' goods is restricted, and great hardship is the consequence. Technological progress frequently results in more unemployment rather than in an easing of the burden of work for all. The profit motive, in conjunction with competition among capitalists, is responsible for an instability in the accumulation and utilization of capital which leads to increasingly severe depressions. Unlimited competition leads to a huge waste of labor, and to that crippling of the social consciousness of individuals which I mentioned before.

Why Socialism?

This crippling of individuals I consider the worst evil of capitalism. Our whole educational system suffers from this evil. An exaggerated competitive attitude is inculcated into the student, who is trained to worship acquisitive success as a preparation for his future career.

I am convinced there is only *one* way to eliminate these grave evils, namely through the establishment of a socialist economy, accompanied by an educational system which would be oriented toward social goals. In such an economy, the means of production are owned by society itself and are utilized in a planned fashion. A planned economy, which adjusts production to the needs of the community, would distribute the work to be done among all those able to work and would guarantee a livelihood to every man, woman, and child. The education of the individual, in addition to promoting his own innate abilities, would attempt to develop in him a sense of responsibility for his fellow men in place of the glorification of power and success in our present society.

Nevertheless, it is necessary to remember that a planned economy is not yet socialism. A planned economy as such may be accompanied by the complete enslavement of the individual. The achievement of socialism requires the solution of some extremely difficult socio-political problems: how is it possible, in view of the far-reaching centralization of political and economic power, to prevent bureaucracy from becoming all-powerful and overweening? How can the rights of the individual be protected and therewith a democratic counterweight to the power of bureaucracy be assured?

Clarity about the aims and problems of socialism is of greatest significance in our age of transition. Since, under present circumstances, free and unhindered discussion of these problems has come under a powerful taboo, I consider the foundation of this magazine to be an important public service.

Albert Einstein, Radical:
A Political Profile

John J. Simon

2005 marks the fiftieth anniversary of the death of Albert Einstein and the centennial of the publication of five of his major scientific papers that transformed the study of physics. Einstein's insights were so revolutionary that they challenged not only established doctrine in the natural sciences, but even altered the way ordinary people saw their world. By the 1920s he had achieved international popular renown on a scale that would not become usual until the rise of the contemporary celebrity saturated tabloids and cable news channels. His recondite scientific papers as well as interviews with the popular press were front page news and fodder for the newsreels. Usually absent, however, was any sober discussion of his participation in the political life of his times as an outspoken radical—especially in profiles and biographies after his death.

Albert Einstein was born on March 14, 1879, into a liberal, secular, and bourgeois German Jewish family. Young Albert's childhood and early adolescence does not seem to have been out of the ordinary. Like many late nineteenth century young men, he was curious, read Darwin, and was interested in the material, that is the natural, world and wished to fathom "the *arcana* of nature, so as to discern 'the law within the law.'"

In 1895, Einstein, aged sixteen, renounced his German citizenship and moved to Switzerland. His main reason was to avoid military service and also to complete his education at Zürich's Polytechnic Institute. There he eventually earned his Ph.D. in a climate relatively free of the anti-Semitism that pervaded German and Austrian universities. But Zürich had other rewards. Einstein spent much time at the Odeon Café, a hangout for Russian radicals, including Alexandra Kollontai and, a few years later, Lenin and Leon Trotsky. Einstein admitted to spending much time at the Odeon, even missing classes to participate in the coffee shop's intoxicating political debates.

Unable to find an academic job, Einstein went to work in 1902 in the Swiss patent office in Berne. It was there in 1905 that he had his *annus mirabilus*, publishing articles on the special theory of relativity, quantum mechanics, and Brownian motion. In 1914 he was offered and accepted a full professorship in Berlin. Fred Jerome, author of *The Einstein File*,[1] notes that the job offer was probably a result of a bidding competition among universities in Britain, France, and Germany looking for scientific and technological talent to abet their respective governments' imperial objectives. Unfortunately, Einstein took up his post just as the First World War broke out with Germany among the chief belligerents.

Einstein opposed the war, putting him at odds with the German Social Democrats to whom he had been previously sympathetic, instead aligning himself with the party's minority who saw the war as a dispute among the ruling classes of the belligerents. Einstein also found himself in disagreement with most of his scientific colleagues. Max Planck, then a physicist of roughly equivalent stature to Einstein, and nearly a hundred other scientists signed a supernationalist "Manifesto to the Civilized World," endorsing Germany's war aims in language that prefigured the Nazi rants of a generation later, rationalizing the war as justifiable resistance to "Russian hordes," "Mongols," and "Negroes" who had been "unleashed against the white race." Einstein and only three others replied in a document suppressed at the time by the German government, describing the behavior of the scientists (sadly joined by numerous writers and artists) as shameful. At least one of the signatories of the reply was jailed. Einstein was not; it was the first instance of the power of his newly acquired celebrity not only to protect himself, but to allow him to speak out when others couldn't.

In the turbulent aftermath of the war Einstein continued to speak out. Famously, on the day Kaiser Wilhelm abdicated—it was during a fortnight that saw not only the armistice, but the fall of seven other European monarchies, all replaced, for the moment, by liberal and socialist regimes—Einstein posted a sign on his classroom's door that read "CLASS CANCELLED—REVOLUTION." He had joined with and defended liberal and radical students and colleagues for their wartime opposition; now he was with them in their postwar resistance to the burgeoning *revanchist* militarism that would quickly morph into Nazism.

Einstein's visibility made him a focus of the revival of virulent anti-Semitism. His work on relativity was denounced as a "Jewish perversion" not only by far right-wing politicians, but even by fellow German scientists. Einstein was by now an illustrious international figure. In 1921 he received the Nobel Prize for Physics for work on the photo-electric effect, which demonstrated the quantum nature of light. He was also a visible presence in the cultural and social life of the Weimar Republic. At the same time, Einstein became increasingly outspoken in his political views. Opposing the mounting racist and jingoist violence and ultranationalism in Germany in the 1920s, he worked for European unity and supported organizations seeking to protect Jews against growing anti-Semitic violence. His egalitarian streak was irrepressible: confronting rising course fees poorer students couldn't afford, Einstein routinely offered free after-hours physics classes. As the European economic and political crises grew more acute, Einstein increasingly used platforms at scientific conferences to address political questions. "He had no problem," Jerome notes, "discussing relativity at a university lecture in the morning, and, on that same evening, urging young people to refuse military service."

By 1930 Hitler's National Socialist party was poised to become the dominant political force in Germany and Einstein, while still vocal at home, more and more found himself looking abroad for congenial outlets for both his scientific and political expression. He lectured in Britain, the Netherlands and elsewhere in Europe and, from 1930 on, annually as a visiting professor at the California Institute of Technology. On January 30, 1933, the Nazis seized power and confiscated Einstein's Berlin property. In May, Goebbels, Hitler's propaganda minister, organized a public book burning, prominently featuring Einstein's work; photos of the atrocity were published worldwide. Following the offer of a large cash bounty for his murder in Nazi newspapers, Einstein was forced to complete a speaking tour in the Netherlands with the protection of bodyguards. That winter, while at Cal Tech, he and his family decided not to return to Berlin. Instead he accepted a lifetime appointment from the Institute for Advanced Study in Princeton, New Jersey, settling into a modest house on Mercer Street.

There, while trying to orient himself to his new country, Einstein worked doggedly on his Unified Field Theory, an attempt to demonstrate that electromagnetism and gravity were different manifestations of a single fundamental phenomenon. It would be his main scientific concern for the rest of his life and remains one that continues to animate contemporary physics and cosmology.

In the years before he was granted U.S. citizenship in 1940, Einstein's political concerns were focused on the depredations of Nazi anti-Semitism and the rise of fascism. Once again, making use of his renown, he petitioned the government to allow refugees to migrate to the United States, but to no avail. He then joined with other European intellectuals to ask Eleanor Roosevelt to intervene with her husband, but the result was the same. This was not Einstein's first conflict with FDR's administration. He vigorously and publicly supported the anti-Franco forces in the Spanish Civil War. While the Nazi Luftwaffe bombed Spanish villages, the United States, along with Britain and France, enforced a phony "neutrality" embargo, denying Republican troops needed munitions. Despite organized demonstrations and appeals to which Einstein lent his name, the blockade was never lifted and the fascist regime imposed on Spain survived (with postwar U.S. aid) for nearly four decades. Nearly 3,000 American volunteers of the Abraham Lincoln Brigade defied their government to fight with the Republic, with Einstein an early and zealous supporter.

In 1939, at the urging of the physicist and fellow refugee from the Nazis, Leo Szilard, Einstein wrote to President Roosevelt to warn about German advances in nuclear research and the prospect that they might develop an atomic weapon. The letter led to the U.S. effort to build such a bomb. It remains Einstein's most remembered public act. However, a combination of government fear of Einstein's radicalism and his own reluctance kept Einstein from having any role in the Manhattan Project. After the war, Einstein protested the incineration of Hiroshima and Nagasaki. Fred Jerome cites a 1946 interview with the London *Sunday Express*, in which Einstein "blamed the atomic bombing of Japan on [President] Truman's anti-Soviet foreign policy" and expressed the opinion that "if FDR had lived through the war, Hiroshima would never have been bombed." Jerome notes that the interview was immediately added to Einstein's growing FBI file.

The early postwar years were marked by a manipulated anticommunist frenzy in government and business circles to support U.S. international and domestic goals. Manhattan Project scientists, who had earlier debated the use of the bomb in the months between Germany's defeat in May 1945 and the Hiroshima bombing in August, were well versed in the issues the bomb raised. Many feared a nuclear arms race between the United States and the Soviet Union. To lobby against that prospect, they founded the Emergency Committee of Atomic Scientists (ECAS), which Einstein agreed to chair. In that role, Einstein sought first to try to meet with Secretary of State George C. Marshall to discuss what he saw as the militarist expansion of U.S. power. He was rebuffed, but in an interview with a mid-level Atomic Energy Commission official he described Truman's foreign policy as anti-Soviet expansionism—*Pax Americana* were the words he used to describe what he saw as U.S. imperial ambition. There was a substantial public response to ECAS's antinuclear message, but, in the end, the group was unable to reach its goal of removing atomic development from the military and placing it under international control.

Another major political concern of Einstein in the 1940s was the persistence of racism, segregation, lynching, and other manifestations of white supremacy in the United States. During the war, the country had been mobilized to support the war effort, both on the battlefield and the home front with the promise of equality. In fact, however, the official message on racial justice was, at best, mixed. FDR set up a Fair Employment Practices Committee, an entity with much promise but with little power to affect discrimination in the work place. And the eleven million member-strong military remained segregated. In the aftermath of the war, economic dislocations, job shifts, and housing shortages were all dealt with in the usual Jim Crow manner: in the words of Leadbelly's song "if you're black, get back, get back, get back." The town of Princeton, New Jersey, where Einstein lived (and for that matter, its university), though only a short drive from New York, might well have been in the old southern Confederacy. Paul Robeson, who was born in Princeton, called it a "Georgia plantation town." Access to housing, jobs, and the university itself (once led by the segregationist Woodrow Wilson) were routinely denied to African Americans; protest or defiance were often met with police violence. Einstein, who had witnessed similar scenes in Germany and who, in any event was a longtime anti-racism militant, reacted against every outrage. In 1937, when the contralto Marion Anderson gave a critically acclaimed concert in Princeton but was denied lodging at the segregated Nassau Inn, Einstein, who had attended the performance, instantly invited her to stay at his house. She did so, and continued to be his guest whenever she sang in New Jersey, even after the hotel was integrated.

In 1946, in the face of a major nationwide wave of lynching, Paul Robeson invited Einstein to join him as co-chair of the American Crusade to End Lynching. The group, which also included W. E. B. Du Bois and others in the civil rights movement, held a rally in Washington at which Einstein was scheduled to speak. Illness prevented that, but he wrote a letter to President Truman calling for prosecution of lynchers, passage of a federal anti-lynching law, and the ouster of racist Mississippi Senator Theodore G. Bilbo. The letter was delivered by Robeson, but the meeting was cut short when he told Truman that if the government would not protect blacks they would have to do so themselves. An uproar followed, but Einstein, in his letter, agreed with Robeson, writing, "There is always a way to overcome legal obstacles whenever there is an inflexible will at work in the service of a just cause."

Einstein was willing to use his fame on behalf of social justice, but steadfastly refused to accept honors his celebrity might have brought his way. There was one exception, however. In May 1946, Horace Mann Bond, president of Lincoln University, a historically black institution in Pennsylvania, awarded the scientist an honorary degree. Einstein accepted, spending the day lecturing to undergraduates and talking, even playing, with faculty children. One of them was Julian Bond, then the young son of the university's president, who later went on to be a leader in the civil rights movement and chair of the NAACP. The press ignored the event, but, in his address Einstein said, "The social outlook of Americans . . . their sense of equality and human dignity is limited to men of white skins. The more I feel an American, the more this situation pains me. I can escape complicity in it only by speaking out." That impulse to political commitment led Einstein to take action on both the domestic crisis in race relations and the simultaneous

Cold War-fostered nuclear menace. It also led him to support the new Progressive Party along with his old compatriot Thomas Mann and his friend and neighbor Ben Shahn—famed for his paintings on the Sacco and Vanzetti case, among many others with political themes. The party, formed by the left wing of Roosevelt's old New Deal coalition, including radicals, socialists, and communists, was established as a vehicle to run former vice president Henry A. Wallace for president in 1948. Einstein especially admired the party's stand against Jim Crow and lent it his prestige and endorsement, being photographed with Wallace and fellow third party supporter Paul Robeson. The latter two campaigning in the South, despite violent attacks on them, refused to appear before segregated audiences or stay in Jim Crow hotels. With Einstein's support, Wallace also called for the international control and outlawing of nuclear weapons. In the end, however, a mix of anti-Soviet jingoism and Truman's belated promises of liberal, New Deal-type social programs caused the collapse of the Wallace movement. Truman's surprise reelection removed whatever barriers to the accelerating Cold War and the ideological repression that accompanied it.

Some among Wallace's supporters chafed at his party's failure to move beyond New Deal liberalism. They thought the party should have taken explicitly socialist positions on questions like public ownership of basic industries, for example. Among those who held such views were

Leo Huberman and Paul M. Sweezy, founders of *Monthly Review* as a venue for ongoing comprehensive analysis and commentary from a socialist and Marxist perspective. Einstein applauded the founding of *Monthly Review*, and, at the request of Huberman's friend Otto Nathan, wrote his essay, "Why Socialism?," for the first issue in May 1949. Together with Einstein's celebrity, the article's clear statement of the case for socialism in logical, moral, and political terms drew attention to the birth of this small left-wing magazine. In the hostile political climate of that time, the article surely provided necessary encouragement both to the authority and the circulation of the new magazine.

At the end of the Second World War Einstein was also drawn to the crisis of European Jewry following the Nazi genocide. Self-identified as a secular Jew, at least since his first encounters with anti-Semitism as a child, he was an intimate observer and intermittent victim of this ultra-nationalist disease and reacted to it as he did to other hate crimes. As early as 1921, when he made his first trip to the United States to raise funds for the establishment of Jewish settlements in Palestine, he sought solutions to the impending catastrophe confronting Europe's Jewish community. He resisted growing legal and extra-legal restrictions on Jewish life in Central and Eastern Europe, supported (with little success) Jewish migration to the Americas, and advocated for the creation of what he and others called a "Jewish national home" in Palestine. As such he was identified with Zionism, a label that does not precisely fit but that he did not actively avoid. Nonetheless, he separated himself from Zionist jingoists and bigots including Vladimir Jabotinsky and Menachem Begin, and often from mainstream Zionists like Chaim Weizmann and David Ben Gurion. In 1930, Einstein wrote, "Oppressive nationalism must be conquered . . . I can see a future for Palestine only on the basis of peaceful cooperation between the two peoples who are at home in the country . . . come together they must in spite of all." He went on to support a binational Jewish and Palestinian state both before and after the war.

In 1946, with hundreds of thousands of European Jews still "displaced" and with the victorious allies unwilling to absorb even a portion of the refugee population, Einstein appeared before an Anglo-American Committee of Inquiry on Palestine, calling for a "Jewish homeland." The Zionist establishment seemed to have intentionally misread this as a call for Jewish sovereignty, so with help from his friend Rabbi Stephen Wise, he clarified his position. Jews, he said, should be able to migrate freely within the limits of the economic absorptive possibilities of Palestine, which in turn should have a government that made sure there was no "'Majorisation' of one group by the other." Resisting Wise's demands for a more forceful statement, Einstein replied that a "rigid demand for a Jewish State will have only undesirable results for us." Radical journalist I. F. Stone praised him for rising above "ethnic limitations." (Einstein later became a charter subscriber to *I. F. Stone's Weekly*.)

Nevertheless, like many Jewish radicals—including many socialists and communists—Einstein had difficulty overcoming his emotional ambivalence about the Zionist project and ultimately applauded Israel's establishment. Given the often inconsistent response of some radicals to Israel's subjugation of Palestinians after the 1967 war, it is difficult to guess how he would have responded. But he was clearly concerned with the implications of Jewish settlement on indigenous Palestinians; it's not much of a stretch to suggest that he would have been appalled by the four decades of oppression of the latter by Israel.

The mid-century "red scare" occupied much of Einstein's last years. He wrote, "The German calamity of years ago repeats itself." Watching Americans lose themselves in the suburbia—and Korean War—driven affluence of the early 1950s, Einstein deplored the fact that "honest people [in the United States] constitute a hopeless minority." But determined to fight back he looked for a forum—and found one in a reply to a 1953 letter from a New York City school teacher who had been fired for his refusal to discuss his politics and name names before a Senate investigating committee. Einstein wrote to William Frauenglass, an innovative teacher who prepared intercultural lessons for his English classes as a way of overcoming prejudicial stereotypes. Einstein exhorted: "Every intellectual who is called before the committees ought to refuse to testify . . . If enough people are ready to take this grave step, they will be successful. If not, then the intellectuals deserve nothing better than the slavery which is intended for them." The letter was national front-page news and had its desired effect. The movement to resist the witch hunt grew stronger. Einstein was supported by voices as distant as that of philosopher Bertrand Russell, who wrote to the *New York Times* from London when they published an editorial disagreeing with Einstein, "Do you condemn the Christian Martyrs who refuse to sacrifice to the Emperor? Do you condemn John Brown?"

Shortly after the Frauenglass affair, another unfriendly witness, Al Shadowitz, told Senator McCarthy that he was refusing to testify saying "I take my advice from Doctor Einstein." McCarthy went ballistic, but, ultimately, the contagion spread both to the Supreme Court, which in 1957 put the brakes on the red hunters (one of the cases involved *Monthly Review* founder Paul Sweezy) and to young New Left students who, beginning in 1960, began to literally break up committee hearings, often with caustic satire and ridicule. It was only ten years after Einstein's letter that Martin Luther King Jr. also employed civil disobedience to fuel the modern civil rights movement.

In 1954, in response to the denial of security clearance to his colleague, the wartime leader of the Manhattan Project, J. Robert Oppenheimer, and other violations of the freedom of scientific inquiry, Einstein wrote, with typical humor, that if he were young again, "I would not try to be a scientist or scholar or teacher, I would rather choose to be a plumber or a peddler, in the hope of finding that modest degree of independence still available under present circumstances."

Einstein also undertook other, more difficult and potentially more dangerous political acts. Perhaps none attracted as much international attention as his effort to intervene in the case against Julius and Ethel Rosenberg. In 1953, Einstein wrote to trial judge Irving Kauffman pointing out that the trial record did not establish the defendants' guilt "beyond a reasonable doubt." He also noted that the scientific evidence against them, even if accurate, did not reveal any vital secret. When he received no response, he wrote to the president with his views. Truman also did not respond, so Einstein released the text of his letter to the media and later wrote to the *New York Times* asking for executive clemency. Tragically, in this circumstance, Einstein's celebrity was to no avail. The Rosenbergs died in Sing Sing's electric chair on June 19.

Two years earlier, in 1951, when his friend W. E. B. Du Bois was indicted for his pro-peace activities on the trumped up charge of being a "Soviet agent," Einstein, along with Robeson and civil rights heroine Mary McLeod Bethune, sponsored a dinner and rally to raise funds for Du

Bois's defense. Du Bois's lawyer, the fiery radical ex-Congressman Vito Marcantonio, managed to reduce the trial to a shambles even before the prosecution had finished its case. But had the trial continued, Marcantonio planned to call Einstein as the first defense witness.

Perhaps no one had been more pilloried or isolated during the "red scare" than Einstein's great ally from the struggle against lynching, Paul Robeson. Attacked as much for his militant stands against white supremacy as for his radicalism and his call for pan-African independence, Robeson had become a virtual non-person in his own country, denied an income, venues for concerts, and the right to travel. In 1952, in a very public act to break the curtain of silence around Robeson, Einstein invited him and his accompanist Lloyd Brown to lunch. The three spent a long afternoon discussing science, music, and politics, all subjects of mutual interest. At one point, when Robeson left the room, Brown remarked about what an honor it was to be in the presence of such a great man. To which Einstein replied, "but it is you who have brought the great man."

Einstein's last years were taken up with both private and public acts of resistance. He used his still considerable network of acquaintance and influence to try to find jobs for those who, like Frauenglass and others, had been fired for non-cooperation with investigating committees. And in 1954 he permitted the celebration of his seventy-fifth birthday to be the occasion for a conference on civil liberties fight-back by the Emergency Civil Liberties Committee (ECLC). The committee had been formed in response to the failure of the American Civil Liberties Union to defend Communists and to take on civil liberties questions raised by the Rosenberg case. The conference, with speakers including I. F. Stone, astronomer and activist Harlow Shapley, sociologists E. Franklin Frazier and Henry Pratt Fairchild, and political scientist H. H. Wilson, launched ECLC on a forty-six-year trajectory defending freedom of expression, the rights of labor, and multifaceted campaigns for civil rights.

It is difficult to know how to conclude this brief and necessarily incomplete summary of Einstein's politics. Not discussed here, for example, are Einstein's lifelong commitments to pacifism and to some sort of world order, nor his long association with the physicist and Marxist Leopold Infeld. Einstein was also deeply committed, as were a number of other left-wing scientists, to mass education in the sciences as a tool against obscurantism and mystical pseudo-science, often used then—and again today—in aid of political and social reaction.

Days before he died on April 18, 1955, Einstein signed what became known as The Einstein-Russell Manifesto. In it, the theoretical physicist and the philosopher-mathematician Bertrand Russell go beyond vague moral arguments for pacifism. Instead they posed political choices:

"There lies before us, if we choose, continual progress in happiness, knowledge, and wisdom. Shall we, instead, choose death, because we cannot forget our quarrels? We appeal as human beings to human beings: Remember your humanity, and forget the rest. If you can do so, the way lies open to a new Paradise; if you cannot, there lies before you the risk of universal death."

Einstein was a radical from his student days until his dying breath. In the last year of his life, ruminating about the political affairs of the day and his world outlook, he told a friend that he remained a "revolutionary," and was still a "fire-belching Vesuvius."

Notes

EINSTEIN'S "WHY SOCIALISM?" AND *MONTHLY REVIEW*:
A HISTORICAL INTRODUCTION

This essay appeared in *Monthly Review* 76 no. 1 (May 2024): 1–23. It
has been slightly revised.

1. Federal Bureau of Investigation, *Albert Einstein*, Part 8 of 14
   (originally numbered 6 of 9) (n.d.), 45 (1002), vault.fbi.gov;
   Fred Jerome, *The Einstein File* (New York: St. Martin's Press,
   2002), 114–15.

2. Federal Bureau of Investigation, *Albert Einstein*, Part 8 of 14
   (originally numbered 6 of 9) (n.d.), 46 (1003); Fred Jerome, *The
   Einstein File* (New York: St. Martin's Press, 2002), 114–15.

3. FBI, *Albert Einstein*, Part 1 of 14 (originally numbered 1 of 9)
   (n.d.), 14; Jerome, *The Einstein File*, 7.

4. Einstein's FBI file continued to refer to his article "Why Socialism?" into the 1950s, relying on information from the anti-Communist American Business Consultants Incorporated, and their
   newsletter, *Counter Attack*. FBI, *Albert Einstein*, Part 9 of 14
   (originally numbered 6 of 9) (n.d.), 82 (1149).

5. Albert Einstein to Franklin D. Roosevelt, August 2, 1939 (letter
   originally drafted by Leo Szilard in consultation with Einstein

and sent to Roosevelt over Einstein's signature), *The Manhattan Project: An Interactive History*, U.S. Department of Energy, osti.gov; Silvan S. Schweber, *Einstein and Oppenheimer* (Cambridge, Massachusetts: Harvard University Press, 2008), 42–46; David E. Rowe and Robert Schulmann, introduction to *Einstein on Politics*, David E. Rowe and Robert Schulmann, eds. (Princeton: Princeton University Press, 2007), 40–41. As Fred Jerome writes: "Einstein blamed the atomic bombings of Japan on Truman's anti Soviet foreign policy…. He told an interviewer from the *Sunday Express* of London that if FDR had lived through the war, Hiroshima never would have been bombed" (Jerome, *The Einstein File*, 56). Einstein's view of the use of the atomic bomb on Japan as the first step in the Cold War was shared by many other scientists at the time, notably the British Nobel Prize-winning nuclear physicist P. M. S. Blackett. See P. M. S. Blackett, *Fear, War, and the Bomb* (New York: McGraw Hill, 1949), 131–39.

6. "Red Visitors Cause Rumpus/The Russians Get a Big Hand from U.S. Friends/Dupes and Fellow Travelers Dress Up Communist Fronts," *Life* 26, no. 14 (April 4, 1949), 39–43; Jerome, *The Einstein File*, 107. Atomic physicist Morrison was to write a regular column on science for *Monthly Review* in the 1950s and early '60s. Radio commentator Walsh was a former Harvard economics instructor and a friend of Sweezy's who wrote for *Monthly Review* in the 1950s.

7. John J. Simon, "Albert Einstein, Radical," *Monthly Review* 57, no. 1 (May 2005): 1–2; "A Coffee House with History," ODEON Zürich, odeon.ch; Ronald W. Clark, *Einstein: The Life and Times* (New York: Harry N. Abrams, 1984), 22.

8. Simon, "Albert Einstein, Radical," 2.

9. Einstein quoted in Rowe and Schulmann, introduction to *Einstein on Politics*, 47.

10. Einstein quoted in Lewis S. Feuer, *Einstein and the Generations of Science* (New York: Basic Books, 1974), 25; Albert Einstein, "On the Fifth Anniversary of Lenin's Death (January 6, 1929)," in *Einstein on Politics*, 413. In writing to Hedwig and Max Born in 1920, Einstein had indicated "I must confess to you that the Bolsheviks do not seem bad to me, however ridiculous their theories." He was particularly impressed by a 1918 work by Karl Radek, whom he saw as an able political figure who knew "his business." Albert Einstein to Hedwig and Max Born, January 27, 1920, in *Einstein on Politics*, 410. Radek later died in Joseph Stalin's purges.

11. Albert Einstein, "The World as I See It" in *Ideas and Opinions* (New York: Crown Publishing, 1954), 8.

12. See Albert Einstein, "'Causality': Lecture at the Marxist Workers School 1930 (Private Notes by Karl Korsch)," translated by Sascha Freyberg and Joost Kircz, *Marxism and the Sciences 3*, no. 1 (Winter 2024): 207–32.

13. Otto Nathan and Heinz Norden, eds., *Einstein on Peace* (New York: Schocken Books, 1960), 180; Rowe and Schulmann, editorial comment in *Einstein on Politics*, 425–27; Albert Einstein to Victor Margueritte, October 19, 1932, in *Einstein on Politics*, 427–28.

14. Albert Einstein, "Is There Room for Individual Freedom in a Socialist State?" in *Einstein on Politics*, 437.

15. Nathan and Norden, introduction to *Einstein on Peace*, viii.

16. Ronald D. Patkus, "The Morris and Adele Bergreen Albert Einstein Collection at Vassar College," *Vassar Encyclopedia* (2005), Archives and Special Collection Library, Vassar College, Poughkeepsie, New York; advertisement, *Vassar Miscellany News*, no. 40, March 24, 1943; "Otto Nathan Dead at 93," *Jewish Telegraphic Agency*, February 3, 1987; Otto Nathan, "Résumé of Dr. Otto Nathan, ca. 1936," W. E. B. Du Bois Papers (MS 312),

Series 1A, Robert S. Cox Special Collections and University Archives, University of Massachusetts Amherst Libraries; Fred Jerome, *Einstein on Israel and Zionism* (New York: St. Martin's Press, 2009), 262. In a 1953 letter from Einstein to Brandeis President Abram L. Sachar quoted by Silvan S. Schweber, Einstein refers to his "closest friend," which in context clearly meant Nathan. Stephen S. Schweber, *Einstein and Oppenheimer* (Cambridge, Massachusetts: Harvard University Press, 2008), 132. See also Jerome, *The Einstein File*, 311.

17. Renee Walsh, "Early Documents of the Formation of Brandeis University," Robert D. Farber University Archive and Special Collections, Brandeis University Library, n.d.; Susan H. Greenberg, "Intellectuals at the Gate, interview with Mark Oppenheimer," *Inside Higher Education*, September 21, 2022.

18. Silvan S. Schweber, "Albert Einstein and the Founding of Brandeis University," in *Revising the Foundations of Relativistic Physics*, A. Ashtekar et al., eds. (Dordrecht: Kluwer Academic Publishers, 2003), 616.

19. Schweber, *Einstein and Oppenheimer,* 112, 117–18.

20. Paul M. Sweezy, *The Theory of Capitalist Development* (New York: Monthly Review Press, 1942, 1972). On Sweezy, see John Bellamy Foster, "The Commitment of an Intellectual: Paul M. Sweezy (1910–2004)," *Monthly Review* 56, no. 5 (October 2004): 5–39.

21. Paul M. Sweezy, oral history interview by Andrew Skotnes, 1986–1987, Columbia Center for Oral History, Columbia University Libraries, 5: 143–44. Harry Magdoff, who was closely associated with *Monthly Review* almost from the beginning, was also well acquainted with Nathan, who visited him at his home (Fred Magdoff, personal communication).

22. Paul M. Sweezy, *A Plan for Brandeis University*, January 1947, 2–10, 18, 44, 87, Albert Einstein Archives (40-461), Hebrew

University of Jerusalem, albert-einstein.huji.ac.il; Otto Nathan, *An Outline of Policy for Brandeis University*, November 9, 1946, Albert Einstein Archives (40-427), Hebrew University of Jerusalem; Schweber, *Einstein and Oppenheimer*, 345; Schweber, "Albert Einstein and the Founding of Brandeis University," in Ashtekar et al., eds., *Revising the Foundations of Relativistic Physics*, 623; Thorstein Veblen, *The Higher Learning in America* (New York: Augustus M. Kelley, 1965). Nathan's five-page outline was closely related to the eighty-seven-page Sweezy plan.

23. Schweber, *Einstein and Oppenheimer*, 119, 122; Leo Huberman and Paul M. Sweezy, "Harold J. Laski," *Monthly Review* 2, no. 1 (May 1950): 5–6.

24. Harold J. Laski, "Why I Am a Marxist," *Monthly Review* 2, no. 3 (July 1950): 81.

25. Schweber, *Einstein and Oppenheimer*, 122–24. In his letter, Laski referred to Nathan, whom he had recently met, as a "good friend."

26. Albert Einstein to Harold J. Laski, April 16, 1947, Harold Joseph Laski Papers, Inventory No. 26.4, International Institute of Social History, Amsterdam. In referring in his letter to Laski to "does not know of discrimination for or against anybody because of sex, color, creed national origin or political opinion," Einstein was using almost the exact same language as employed by Nathan in his *An Outline of Policy for Brandeis University*, while the Sweezy Plan was also almost identical in its wording. See Nathan, *An Outline of Policy for Brandeis University*, 1; Sweezy, *A Plan for Brandeis University*, 3.

27. Schweber, *Einstein and Oppenheimer*, 124.

28. Schweber, *Einstein and Oppenheimer*, 123, 347.

29. "Left Bias Charged in University Row," *New York Times*, June 23, 1947; Schweber, *Einstein and Oppenheimer*, 125–32.

30. "Group Accuses 76 Faculty Members of Red Leanings," *Harvard Crimson*, March 10, 1949; Ben W. Heineman Jr., "The University in the McCarthy Era," *Harvard Crimson*, June 17, 1965.

31. Einstein quoted in Schweber, *Einstein and Oppenheimer*, 129.

32. Schweber, *Einstein and Oppenheimer*, 128–30. Alpert and the first president of Brandeis, Sachar, entered into a power struggle over who was to control the university shortly after Sachar was appointed and Alpert was driven from the board. Schweber, *Einstein and Oppenheimer*, 130–31.

33. Photo of Henry Wallace, Albert Einstein, Frank Kingdon, and Paul Robeson, Wikimedia Commons, commons.wikimedia.org.

34. Karl M. Schmidt, *Henry A Wallace: Quixotic Crusade, 1948* (Syracuse, New York: Syracuse University Press, 1960), 190–91. Harry Magdoff, who was to become co-editor of the magazine with Huberman's death, wrote the small business section of the Progressive Party platform. Sweezy, by virtue of his role in the Wallace campaign and also due to a lecture that he had delivered at the University of New Hampshire, was subpoenaed by the New Hampshire Attorney General in 1954, and was given contempt of court charges when he refused to name the names of members of the Progressive Party, the Communist party, or to turn over his lecture notes. He based his defense (as had Leo Huberman when called before McCarthy's own committee) on the First Amendment, following a strategy advanced by Einstein in 1953. Sweezy's case, *Sweezy v. New Hampshire*, was finally decided by the U.S. Supreme Court in a landmark 1957 decision. John J. Simon, "*Sweezy v. New Hampshire*," *Monthly Review* 51, no. 11 (April 2000): 35–37.

35. Peter Kuznick, "Undoing the New Deal: Truman's Cold War Buries Wallace and the Left," The Real News Network, December 7, 2017.

36. Albert Einstein to John Dudzic, March 8, 1948, in *Einstein on Politics*, 454. Einstein complained about the watering down of the concept of liberalism, which historically had had a very definite meaning in European political discourse, but had become everything and nothing with Roosevelt's use of it as a label for the New Deal. Einstein's misgivings were later confirmed by Wallace's statements on "progressive capitalism" and "liberalism" in two pieces published in *Monthly Review* in 1950: Henry A. Wallace, "What Is Progressive Capitalism?," *Monthly Review* 1, no. 12 (April 1950): 390–94; Henry A. Wallace, "Needed: Cooperation Between the U.S. and the USSR in a Strong UN," *Monthly Review* 2, no. 1 (May 1950): 7–10. See also I. F. Stone, "Problems of the Progressive Party," *Monthly Review* 1, no. 12 (April 1950): 379–89.

37. Sweezy, oral history interview by Skotnes, 5: 143–44; "Interview with Paul M. Sweezy," *Monthly Review* 51, no. 1 (May 1999): 32; John J. Simon, "Paul Sweezy," *Guardian*, March 4, 2004.

38. Christopher Phelps, "Introduction: A Socialist Magazine in the American Century," *Monthly Review* 51, no. 1 (May 1999): 2–3.

39. Sweezy, oral history interview, 5: 143–44; Simon, "Albert Einstein, Radical," 8. Otto Nathan and Paul A. Baran, a central figure in *Monthly Review*'s history, entered into a personal dispute that affected Nathan's relations with Huberman as well, much to his dismay, resulting in a distancing of Nathan from the magazine following its foundation. Sweezy, oral history interview, 5: 144; Robert W. McChesney, "The *Monthly Review* Story: 1949–1984," MR Online, May 6, 2007.

40. An example of this is Scott Nearing, "Why I Believe in Socialism," *Monthly Review* 1, no. 2 (June 1949): 44–50.

41. As John J. Simon noted, as a result of these connections, Einstein was viewed as "part of the extended *MR* [*Monthly Review*] family" (Simon, "*Sweezy v. New Hampshire*," 36).

42. C. Wright Mills, introduction to Thorstein Veblen, *The Theory of the Leisure Class* (New York: Mentor, 1953), vi.

43. Albert Einstein, "Remarks on Bertrand Russell's Theory of Knowledge," in *The Philosophy of Bertrand Russell*, Paul A. Schilpp, ed. (Evanston, Illinois: Library of Living Philosophers, 1944), 279. Einstein's interest in Thorstein Veblen was likely sparked by his acquaintance with the mathematician Ostwald Veblen, who was a colleague of his at Princeton University and who was Veblen's nephew. William T. Ganley, "A Note on the Intellectual Connection Between Albert Einstein and Thorstein Veblen," *Journal of Economic Issues* 31, no. 1 (March 1997): 245–51.

44. Albert Einstein, "The Jewish Community," in *Ideas and Opinions*, 174. In another statement he referred to Moses, Spinoza, and Marx. See Einstein, *Ideas and Opinions*, 195.

45. Einstein's statement that nowhere were there to be found societies outside the "predatory phase" was an admission that complete socialism existed nowhere at the time.

46. Albert Einstein, "Why Socialism?," *Monthly Review* 1, no. 1 (May 1949): 9–10.

47. Einstein, "Why Socialism?," 10.

48. Einstein, "Why Socialism?," 10. Besides "Why Socialism?," Einstein also mentioned in "On Freedom" in 1940 the view of "someone who approves, as a goal, the extirpation of the human race from the earth." This is something, he added, that "one cannot refute . . . on rational grounds," since it removes the basis for rational discussion. Albert Einstein, "On Freedom," in *Ideas and Opinions*, 31–32.

49. Einstein does not tell us what he means by social drives, but there is ample reason to suppose he was intrigued by Veblen's argument in *The Instinct of Workmanship*. Veblen emphasized that what were often called "instincts" were really "tropismat-

ic" drives, arising purely from biological constitutions, which constituted part of human psychology, but which, from a social psychological standpoint, were ultimately less important than the social drives, or social "instincts." Veblen emphasized three primary social drives, constituting the positive elements of human cultural evolution, which he called "the instinct of workmanship" (standing for productive drives), "the parental bent" (reproductive drives), and "idle curiosity" (drives related to the pursuit of knowledge and science). In his view, these social drives were often "contaminated," going against each other, leading to contradictory and ultimately insupportable forms such as the "predatory" and "pecuniary" phases of culture that set individuals against society by accentuating "exploit," "emulation," and egoism. Thorstein Veblen, *The Instinct of Workmanship* (New York: Augustus M. Kelley, 1914), 1–8, 42–44, 157, 175, 205; Thorstein Veblen, *The Place of Science in Modern Civilization* (New York: Russell and Russell, 1961), 395; C. E. Ayres, "Veblen's Theory of Instincts Reconsidered," in *Thorstein Veblen: A Critical Reappraisal* (Ithaca, New York: Cornell University Press, 1958), 28–29.

50. Einstein, "Why Socialism?," 12.

51. Einstein, "Why Socialism?," 10–12.

52. Marx regarded the distinction between labor and *labor power*, to which Einstein refers here, to be one of the most key elements of his political-economic critique. See Karl Marx and Frederick Engels, *Selected Correspondence* (Moscow: Progress Publishers, 1975), 180–81.

53. Einstein, "Why Socialism?," 12–13. See also Albert Einstein, "Thoughts on the World Economic Crisis, (ca. 1930), in *Einstein on Politics*, 415.

54. See also Einstein, "Is There Room for Individual Freedom in a Socialist State?" in *Einstein on Politics*, 437.

55. The reserve army of labor, the role of revolutions in technology in constantly reproducing it, and the associated concentration and centralization of capital—propositions that Einstein relies on here—are all treated by Marx in chapter 25 of the first volume of *Capital*. See Karl Marx, *Capital*, vol. 1 (London: Penguin, 1976), 762–870.

56. Einstein, "Why Socialism?," 13–14.

57. Einstein, "Why Socialism?," 14.

58. Einstein, "Why Socialism?," 14–15.

59. Einstein, "Why Socialism?," 15. All three of the original founders of *Monthly Review*, Sweezy, Huberman, and Nathan, were caught up in the McCarthyite inquisition of the 1950s. In addition to Sweezy's battle, which took him to the U.S. Supreme Court, Huberman was called before McCarthy's own Senate committee. Nathan had his U.S. passport revoked for two and a half years. He was also subpoenaed by the House Un-American Activities Committee. Along with others, such as Paul Robeson and Arthur Miller, he was charged with contempt of court for failure to cooperate. All three (Huberman, Sweezy, and Nathan) stood on the First Amendment, as Einstein had recommended, and refused to name names. Leo Huberman, "A Challenge to the Book Burners (July 14, 1953)," *Monthly Review* 5, no. 4 (August 1953): 158–73; Geoffrey Ryan, "Un-American Activities," *Index on Censorship* 2, no. 3 (September 1973): 90–91; Jerome, *The Einstein File*, 249.

60. See the well-known biography by Ronald Clark, in which Einstein's politics, aside from Zionism, are scarcely visible. Clark, *Einstein: The Life and Times*.

61. Rowe and Schulmann, introduction to *Einstein on Politics*, 55; Fred Jerome and Rodger Taylor, *Einstein on Race and Racism* (New Brunswick, New Jersey: Rutgers University Press, 2005), 8–10, 135–36; Maria Popova, "Albert Einstein's Little-Known

Correspondence with W. E. B. Du Bois About Equality and Radical Justice," *The Marginalian*, January 6, 2015.

62. Rowe and Schulmann, editorial comment in *Einstein on Politics*, 479.

63. Rowe and Schulmann, introduction to *Einstein on Politics*, 47–48, 50.

64. Rowe and Schulmann, editorial comment in *Einstein on Politics*, 408.

65. Einstein, "Is There Room for Individual Freedom in a Socialist State?" in *Einstein on Politics*, 437. Einstein always argued that complete socialism, in the sense in which he understood it, was not to be found in any existing state. Einstein to John Dudzic, March 8, 1948, in *Einstein on Politics*, 454.

66. Rowe and Schulmann, introduction to *Einstein on Politics*, 48; Einstein, "Is There Room for Individual Freedom in a Socialist State?" in *Einstein on Politics*.

67. Rowe and Schulmann, introduction to *Einstein on Politics*, 48–49.

68. Rowe and Schulmann, introduction to *Einstein on Politics*, 49. Albert Einstein, "'Causality': Lecture at the Marxist Workers School" 1930.

69. Rowe and Schulmann, introduction to *Einstein on Politics*, 50, 407.

70. Rowe and Schulmann, introduction to *Einstein on Politics*, 51.

71. Editorial identification of author, Einstein, "Why Socialism?," 9; Rowe and Schulmann, introduction to *Einstein on Politics*, 47.

72. Rowe and Schulmann, editorial comment in *Einstein on Politics*, 438.

73. An example of this is to be found in Arthur H. Reis Jr., "The Albert Einstein Involvement," *Brandeis Review: Fiftieth Anniversary Edition* (1998), 60–61.

74. See Walsh, "Early Documents of the Formation of Brandeis University."

75. Much of Einstein's general outlook on the United States was undoubtedly similar to Veblen's in his 1918 *The Higher Learning in America*, with its strong critique of the "governing boards" of the universities. Veblen, *The Higher Learning in America*, 59–84. Sweezy had included a reference to Veblen's work in his Brandeis plan in support of his own criticisms of such governing boards. See Sweezy, *A Plan for Brandeis University*, 18.

76. Reis, "The Albert Einstein Involvement," 61. Einstein had early on opposed the appointment of Sachar as president of Brandeis, as pushed at that time by Israel Goldstein, then chairman of both the Albert Einstein Foundation and the Board of Trustees. In the course of the dispute, Goldstein resigned both positions and was replaced by Lazrus as chairman of the Foundation and Alpert as chairman of the Board of Trustees.

77. Jerome and Taylor, *Einstein on Race and Racism*, 88–94, 139–42; Simon, "Albert Einstein, Radical," 6–7; Fred Jerome, *The Einstein File*, 79–85.

78. Jerome and Taylor, *Einstein on Race and Racism*, 119–20.

79. On Marcantonio, see John J. Simon, "Rebel in the House: The Life and Times of Vito Marcantonio," *Monthly Review* 57, no. 11 (April 2006): 24–46; Richard Sasuly, "Vito Marcantonio: The People's Politician," in *American Radicals*, Harvey Goldberg, ed. (New York: Monthly Review Press, 1957), 145–59.

80. Shirley Graham Du Bois quoted in Jerome and Taylor, *Einstein on Race and Racism*, 121.

81. Jerome and Taylor, *Einstein on Race and Racism*, 119–21; Simon, "Albert Einstein, Radical," 10–11. On W. E. B. Du Bois's views on U.S. capitalism in the 1950s, see W. E. B. Du Bois, "Negroes and the Crisis of Capitalism in the U.S.," *Monthly Review* 4, no. 12 (April 1953): 478–85.

82. Albert Einstein to the Queen Mother of Belgium, January 2, 1955, in *Einstein on Peace*, 615–16; Albert Einstein to Eugene Rabinowitch, January 5, 1951, in *Einstein on Peace*, 553. There is little doubt that Einstein was familiar with major critical analyses of the Korean War. *Monthly Review* published assessments of the war from the outset. I. F. Stone's *The Hidden History of the Korean War*, launching Monthly Review Press, was published in 1952. The following year Einstein became a charter subscriber to Stone's *I. F. Stone Weekly*. Simon, "Albert Einstein, Radical," 9.

83. Fred Jerome, *Einstein on Israel and Zionism* (New York: St. Martin's Press, 2009), 225–32.

84. Samuel Graydon, "Einstein's Complicated Relationship to Judaism," *Time*, December 19, 2023.

85. Albert Einstein, "Our Debt to Zionism," in *Einstein on Politics*, 301; Albert Einstein, "Testimony at a Hearing of the Anglo-American Committee of Inquiry, January 11, 1946," in *Einstein on Politics*, 344–45; Jerome, *Einstein on Israel and Zionism*, 4, 29–30.

86. Yorgos Mitralis, "When Einstein Called 'Fascists' Those Who Ruled Israel for the Last 44 Years," Committee for the Abolition of Illegitimate Debt, October 31, 2023; Isidore Abramowitz, Hannah Arendt, Abraham Brick, Jessurun Cardozo, Albert Einstein, et al., Letter to the *New York Times*, December 4, 1948, marxists.org.

87. "Israel-Gaza War in Maps and Charts: Live Tracker," *Al Jazeera*, accessed April 5, 2024.

88. Jerome, *The Einstein File*, 62–68; "Dear Professor Einstein: The Emergency Committee of Atomic Scientists in Post-War America," Oregon State University archives, scarc.library.oregonstate.edu.

89. John Bellamy Foster, *The Return of Nature* (New York: Monthly Review Press, 2020), 502–3; *Einstein on Peace*, 590, 593, 605.

90. Bertrand Russell, Albert Einstein, et al., "Russell-Einstein Manifesto," in *Einstein on Peace*, 632–35.

91. Einstein, "Is There Room for Individual Freedom in a Socialist State?" in *Einstein on Politics*, 438; Einstein, "Human Rights (February 20, 1954)," in *Einstein on Politics*, 497.

92. Steven Schultz, "Newly Discovered Diary Chronicles Einstein's Last Years," *Princeton Weekly Bulletin* 93, no. 25, April 26, 2004; Simon, "Albert Einstein, Radical," 12.

ALBERT EINSTEIN, RADICAL: A POLITICAL PROFILE

This essay first appeared in *Monthly Review* 57 no. 1 (May 2005): 1–12.

1. Fred Jerome, *The Einstein File: J. Edgar Hoover's Secret War Against the World's Most Famous Scientist* (New York: Saint Martin's Press/Griffin, 2002); see also Fred Jerome, "The Hidden Half-Life of Albert Einstein: Anti-Racism," in *Socialism and Democracy* 18, no. 2 (http://www.sdonline.org/33/fred_jerome.htm).

   Jerome's important work uses the huge FBI-compiled file on Einstein, not only to expose Hoover's machinations as well as the covert mechanisms and techniques of character assassination, but as a vehicle to introduce readers to the much hidden activist radical and socialist the scientist was. Fred Jerome and Rodger Taylor, *Einstein On Race and Racism* (New Brunswick, N.J.: Rutgers University Press, 2006).

   Two useful biographies are: Jeremy Bernstein, *Einstein* (New York: Viking Press, 1973); and Ronald W. Clark, *Einstein: The Life and Times* (New York: Avon Books, 1984), the standard biography, but with almost no mention of Einstein's politics other than Zionism.

Books by Einstein for the general reader include: *Ideas and Opinions* (New York: Three Rivers Press, 1995); *The World As I See It* (New York: Citadel Press, 1993); *Out of My Later Years* (New York: Gramercy Books, 1993); and (with Leopold Infeld) *The Evolution of Physics* (New York: Free Press, 1967), still the most accessible and the best description of the progression from Newtonian to modern quantum mechanics and relativity.

Index

Index

Index

Index

Index